A. Hugh Fisher

The Cathedral Church of Hereford,

A Description of its Fabric and a Brief History of the Episcopal See

A. Hugh Fisher

The Cathedral Church of Hereford,
A Description of its Fabric and a Brief History of the Episcopal See

ISBN/EAN: 9783744716864

Printed in Europe, USA, Canada, Australia, Japan

Cover: Foto ©Andreas Hilbeck / pixelio.de

More available books at **www.hansebooks.com**

Photochrom Co., Ld., Photo.]

HEREFORD FROM THE WYE.

THE CATHEDRAL CHURCH OF
HEREFORD

A DESCRIPTION OF ITS FABRIC AND A BRIEF HISTORY OF THE EPISCOPAL SEE

BY

A. HUGH FISHER

WITH FORTY  ILLUSTRATIONS

LONDON GEORGE BELL & SONS 1898

GENERAL PREFACE.

THIS series of monographs has been planned to supply visitors to the great English Cathedrals with accurate and well illustrated guide-books at a popular price. The aim of each writer has been to produce a work compiled with sufficient knowledge and scholarship to be of value to the student of Archæology and History, and yet not too technical in language for the use of an ordinary visitor or tourist.

To specify all the authorities which have been made use of in each case would be difficult and tedious in this place. But amongst the general sources of information which have been almost invariably found useful are : — (1) the great county histories, the value of which, especially in questions of genealogy and local records, is generally recognised ; (2) the numerous papers by experts which appear from time to time in the Transactions of the Antiquarian and Archæological Societies ; (3) the important documents made accessible in the series issued by the Master of the Rolls ; (4) the well-known works of Britton and Willis on the English Cathedrals ; and (5) the very excellent series of Handbooks to the Cathedrals, originated by the late Mr. John Murray ; to which the reader may in most cases be referred for fuller detail, especially in reference to the histories of the respective sees.

GLEESON WHITE.
EDWARD F. STRANGE.
Editors of the Series.

AUTHOR'S PREFACE.

In addition to the well-known books mentioned in the General Preface, the "Monastic Chronicles" and many other works named in the text, some dealing especially with Hereford have been of valuable assistance to me in preparing this little book. Amongst these are the various careful studies of the Rev. Francis Havergal, Dean Merewether's exhaustive "Statement of the Condition and Circumstances of the Cathedral Church of Hereford in the Year 1841," and "The Diocese of Hereford," by the Rev. H. W. Phillott.

My best thanks are also due to the Photochrom Company for their excellent photographs.

A. HUGH FISHER.

CONTENTS.

	PAGE
CHAPTER I.—History of the Building	3
CHAPTER II.—Exterior	26
The Central Tower	27
Bishop Booth's Porch	28
The North Transept	28
The Lady Chapel	29
The Bishops' Cloisters	30
The Chapter-House	30
The Vicars' Cloisters	32
CHAPTER III.—Interior	34
The Nave	34
The Screen	38
The Central Tower	41
The North Transept	43
The South Transept	51
The Bishops' Cloisters	56
The South-East Transept	57
The Lady Chapel	59
The Audley Chantry	66
The Crypt	67
The Vicars' Cloisters	68
The North-East Transept	69
The Choir	74
The Choir Stalls	79
The Cathedral Library	80
Reliquary of St Thomas of Canterbury	84
Ancient Gold Rings	86
The Stained Glass	87
CHAPTER IV.—History of the See	90
Dimensions of the Cathedral	112

ILLUSTRATIONS.

	PAGE
Hereford from the Wye	*Frontispiece*
Arms of Hereford	*Title*
Hereford Cathedral, from the South-East	2
Gargoyles in the Cloisters	13, 93, 108, 109
The Audley Chapel	16
The West Front, from an old print	19
The Nave after the fall of the West End	21
The Cathedral, from the North, at the end of the Seventeenth Century	23
Bishop Booth's Porch and North Transept	27
General View, from the West	29
Exterior of the Lady Chapel	31
The Cloisters, with the Ladies' Arbour	33
The North Porch	35
The Nave	37
The Choir Screen	39
Section through Tower and Transepts	40
North Arch of Central Tower, showing Masonry erected about 1320	43
The North Transept	45
The Cantilupe Shrine	49
East Wall of the South Transept	53
The Lady Chapel	60
Section through Lady Chapel and Crypt	61
Arch discovered at Entrance of Lady Chapel	62
Seal of Johanna de Bohun	64
The Crypt	67
View behind the Altar, looking North	71
Compartment of Choir, Exterior, North Side	74
Compartment of Choir, Interior, North Side	75
East End of the Choir in 1841	77
Early English Window Moulding	79
The Reredos	81
Ancient Reliquary in the Cathedral	85
Monumental Crocket	88
Early English Basement Moulding	88
Tomb of Bishop Thos. Charleton	99
Bye Street Gate, from an old print	110
PLAN	111

B

HEREFORD CATHEDRAL, FROM THE SOUTH-EAST.

Photochrom Co., Ld., Photo.

HEREFORD CATHEDRAL.

CHAPTER I.

THE HISTORY OF THE BUILDING.

THE early history of Hereford, like that of the majority of cathedral churches, is veiled in the obscurity of doubtful speculation and shadowy tradition. Although the see had existed from the sixth century, it is not till much later that we have any information concerning the cathedral itself.

From 755 to 794 there reigned in Mercia one of the most powerful and important rulers of those times,—King Offa. He was a contemporary of Charles the Great, and more than once these two sovereigns exchanged gifts and letters. Under Offa Mercia became the first power in Britain, and in addition to much fighting with the West Saxons and the Kentish men he wrested a large piece of the country lying west of the Severn from the Welsh, took the chief town of the district which was afterwards called Shrewsbury, and like another Severus made a great dyke from the mouth of the Wye to that of the Dee which became henceforth the boundary between Wales and England, a position it has held with few changes to the present day. In church history Offa is of no less importance than in secular, for as the most powerful King in England he seems to have determined that ecclesiastical affairs in this country should be more under his control, or at least supervision, than they could possibly be with the Mercian church subject to the Archbishop of Canterbury. In 786, therefore, he persuaded the Pope to create the Archbishopric of Lichfield.

Although Canterbury regained its supremacy upon Offa's death when Lichfield was shorn by a new Pope of its recently acquired honours, the position gained for the latter see by Offa, though temporary in itself, must have had lasting and important influence. Offa is generally held responsible for the murder, about 793, of Æthelberht, King of the East Angles, who had been promised his daughter, Æthelthryth, in marriage.

Had Æthelberht been gifted with a knowledge of future events (which would not have been a more wonderful attribute than many of the virtues which were ascribed afterwards to his dead body), he could hardly have desired a more glorious fate. His murder gained for him martyrdom with its immortal glory, and he could scarce have met his death under happier auspices. Visiting a king's residence to fetch his bride he died by the order of a man whose memory is sullied by no other stain, a man renowned in war, a maker of laws for the good of his people, and eminent in an ignorant age as one who encouraged learning.

Legend and tradition have so obscured this event that beyond the bare fact of the murder nothing can be positively asserted, and the brief statement of the Anglo-Saxon Chronicle, "792. This year Offa, King of the Mercians, commanded the head of King Æthelberht to be struck off," contains all that we may be certain of.

One writer speaks of a hired assassin, and others lay the crime at the door of Cynethryth, Offa's Queen, who is said to have insinuated that the marriage was only sought as a pretext to occupy the Mercian throne. Finding her lord's courage not equal to the occasion, she herself arranged the end of Æthelberht. There is talk of a pit dug in his sleeping-chamber and a chair arranged thereover, which, with an appearance of luxurious comfort, lured him to his fate. The body was, according to one writer, privately buried on the bank of the river "Lugg," near Hereford.

"On the night of his burial," says the Monkish Annalist, "a column of light, brighter than the sun, arose towards heaven"; and three nights afterwards the figure (or ghost) of King Æthelberht appeared to Brithfrid, a nobleman, and commanded him to convey the body to a place called "Stratus Waye," and to inter it near the monastery there. Guided by another column of light, Brithfrid, having placed the body and the

THE HISTORY OF THE BUILDING.

head on a carriage, proceeded on his journey. The head fell from the vehicle, but having been discovered by a "blind man," to whom it miraculously communicated sight, was restored by him to the careless driver. Arrived at his place of destination, then called "Fernlega" or "Saltus Silicis," and which has since been termed Hereford, he there interred the body. Whatever the motive for the crime, there is ample evidence of Offa's subsequent remorse. In atonement he built monasteries and churches, and is even said by some to have gone on a pilgrimage to Rome, though this rests on slight evidence.

The miracles worked at the tomb of the murdered King were, according to Asser, so numerous and incredible that Offa, who had appropriated Æthelberht's kingdom, was induced to send two bishops to Hereford to ascertain the truth of them, and it is generally agreed that about A.D. 825 Milfrid, who was Viceroy to the Mercian King Egbert after the death of Offa and of his son Egfrid, expended a large sum of money in building "*Ecclesiam egregiam, lapidea structura*" at Hereford, which he consecrated to the martyred monarch, and endowed with lands and enriched with ornaments.

Although one of the old chroniclers calls it a church of stone, it is quite uncertain what were the materials, size, or architectural character of this edifice. It seems, however, that by 1012, when Bishop Athelstan was promoted to the see, it had fallen into sheer ruin, or, at any rate, sufficient decay to necessitate his beginning a new building. Of this no clearer account has been handed down to us than of Milfrid's church. Soon after it was finished Algar or Elfgar, Earl of Chester, son of the Earl of Mercia, was charged with treason at a Witan in London, and (though his guilt is still disputed) was outlawed by Edward the Confessor. He hired a fleet of Danish pirate ships from the Irish coast, joined King Gruffydd in Wales, and marched with him into Herefordshire, determining to make war upon King Edward. Here they began with a victory about two miles from Hereford over the Earl of that shire who was a Frenchman, and tried to make his men fight on horseback in the French fashion, which they did not understand,—the English way being for the great men to ride to the field of battle, but there to dismount and fight with their heavy axes on foot. Earl Ralph, the Frenchman, turned his horse's head and fled the field, and the English, encumbered with their long spears and swords, followed helter skelter. After killing some five hundred, Ælfgar and Gruffydd turned to Hereford and came upon the church which Bishop Athelstan had caused to be built. There they met with a spirited resistance: amongst other victims seven of the canons were killed in an attempt to hold the great door of the minster; but, ultimately, the church and town were burned.

Earl Harold, son of Earl Godwin, himself, when it was too late, came with half of his army to Hereford, and with his usual predilection for peace (notwithstanding his valour) soon after removed the outlawry from Ælfgar, and quiet was restored.

In 1056, the year following this disaster, the worthy Bishop Athelstan died at Bosbury. He had been blind for thirteen years before his death, and a Welsh bishop had acted for him. His body was interred in the church which he had "built from the foundations," and we may therefore suppose that the "minster" was not entirely destroyed.

In 1057, on the death of Earl Ralph, the Frenchman, so important was Herefordshire, through its position on the Welsh borders, and, since it had been strengthened by Harold, such an important military post was the town of Hereford, that it became part of his earldom.

From 1055 to 1079 the minster is said to have been in ruins. At the latter date Bishop Lozing (Robert de Losinga) began to rebuild the cathedral, and there are vague accounts that it was in the form of a round church in imitation of a basilica of Charlemagne which had been built at Aix-la-Chapelle between 774 and 795. If such a form ever existed it must have been completely destroyed, as the work of the Norman period that remains is clearly English both in treatment and in detail. If this could be proved to be Lozing's work, then it had no similarity to the Roman style. The building begun by him was carried on by Bishop Raynelm, who held the see from 1107 to 1115, and placed on a more regular basis the establishment of canons living under a rule. These prebendaries or canons did not live in common like the monks, but in separate houses near the church. Whether he completed the building or not, Bishop Raynelm undoubtedly made many additions and alterations.

We may here quote an interesting account of the duties of

the cathedral treasurer, which were probably settled about this time. They throw a curious and suggestive light on the ceremonies of the period. "At Hereford," says Walcott, "he found all the lights; three burning day and night before the high altar; two burning there at matins daily, and at mass, and the chief hours on festivals; three burning perpetually, viz., in the chapter-house, the second before S. Mary's altar, and the third before the cross in the rood-loft; four before the high altar, and altar on "*Minus Duplicia*," and five tapers in basons, on principles, and doubles, at mass, prime, and second vespers, four tapers before the high altar, five in the basons, thirteen on the beam, and seven in the candelabra; the paschal and portable tapers for processions. He kept the keys of the treasury, copes, palls, vestments, ornaments, and the plate, of which he rendered a yearly account to the dean and chapter. He found three clerks to ring the bells, light the candles, and suspend the palls and curtains on solemn days. He found hay at Christmas to strew the choir and chapter-house, which at Easter was sprinkled with ivy leaves; and on All Saints' day he provided mats."[1]

The next great changes were made under Bishop William de Vere (1186–1199). His work was of transitional character, and bears much resemblance to the beautiful transitional work at Glastonbury. He removed the three Norman apsidal terminations at the east end, doubled the presbytery aisles, thus making two side chapels in each transept which have since been replaced by the Lady Chapel with its vestibule.

In a paper read before the Archæological Institute in 1877, Sir G. G. Scott suggests that the central apse projected one bay beyond the sides; but this is merely conjecture. A curious feature in De Vere's work was his putting columns in the middle of the central arch. It is probable that the part of the presbytery we now have was but the beginning of a larger scheme never carried out, which included building the presbytery and dividing the eastern wall into two arches instead of one as at Lichfield and Exeter.

According to Sir Gilbert Scott's theory, the Early English Lady Chapel was an extension of the work of Bishop de Vere: it is especially interesting, and an unique example of its date in being raised upon a crypt.

[1] *Cathedralia*, p. 59.

At the Bishop's palace was a splendid hall of which it seems likely De Vere was the builder,—at any rate he must have been the first or second occupier. It was of noble dimensions, being 110 feet in length, consisting of a nave 23 feet broad, with aisles 16 feet wide, independently of the columns. This was divided into five bays by pillars supporting timber arches formed of two pieces of curved oak. Nearly the whole of the present Bishop's palace is included within the space occupied by this grand hall.

In 1188 when Archbishop Baldwin made pilgrimage into Wales on behalf of the crusade, he was entertained in this hall by Bishop de Vere, and doubtless some of those who devoted themselves to the work were Hereford men.

The central tower of the cathedral, that fine example of decorated work, covered with its profusion of ball-flower ornament, was built by, or at any rate during the episcopate of, Giles de Braose (1200-1215), an ardent opponent of King John.

The remaining examples of decorated date are the inner north porch (as distinct from the addition of Bishop Booth) and what remains of the beautifully designed chapter-house, a decagon in plan, each side except the one occupied by the entrance being subdivided into five seats.

During the term of office of Bishop Foliot (1219-1234), a tooth of St. Æthelberht, whose remains had been almost entirely destroyed by Ælfgar and Gruffuth in 1055, was given to the cathedral. The donor of this precious relic was Philip de Fauconberg, Canon of Hereford and Archdeacon of Huntingdon.

The next Bishop, Ralph de Maydenstan, 1234-1239, presented some service-books to the cathedral.

In 1240 Henry III., with his wonted preference for foreigners, appointed to the Hereford bishopric, Peter of Savoy, generally known as Bishop Aquablanca, from Aqua Bella, his birthplace, near Chambéry. He it was who rebuilt the north transept. He was one of the best hated men in England, and not content with showering benefices upon his relations, he perpetrated one of the greatest frauds in history in order to raise money to aid the annexation schemes of Popes Innocent IV. and Alexander IV. Of these, however, full particulars will be found in a chapter on the Diocese.

While he was absent in Ireland collecting tithes, attended

THE HISTORY OF THE BUILDING.

by a guard of soldiers, Prince Edward, coming to Hereford to resist the encroachments of Llewellyn, King of Wales, found there neither bishop, dean, nor canons resident. For this they earned the severe reprimand of the King, and the Bishop returned to Hereford. Shortly after, he was seized within the cathedral precincts by the insurgent barons of Leicester's party, together with all the foreign canons (who were his own relations). They were carried to Eardisley Castle, where the spoil they had just brought from Ireland was divided among the insurgents.

Bishop Aquablanca died soon after these events, in 1268. He was endowed with a character full of contradictions, extreme aggressiveness, mingled with remarkable tact.

When he got the better of the Hereford citizens, after their attempt to encroach upon his episcopal rights, he remitted one full half of their fine and devoted the other to the cathedral building. While he was showing in his life a disgraceful example to the clergy of the country, at the same time he gave liberally to the cathedral foundation in books, ornaments, money, and land, left a rich legacy to the poor, and a lasting monument in the rebuilding of the north transept of the cathedral itself.

With the exception of the arches, leading into the aisles of the nave and choir, the Norman work of the transept was altogether demolished, and replaced by another consisting of two bays with an eastern aisle. Over the latter was built a story now used as the cathedral library, which is approached from the north aisle of the presbytery by a staircase turret. His tomb is one of the finest in the cathedral. Under it, together with those of his nephew, a Dean of Hereford, are his own remains, except the heart, which, as he had wished, was carried to his own country of Savoy.

In 1275 the Chapter of Hereford elected to the bishopric Thomas de Cantilupe, one of the greatest men who has ever held that office, a man whose life was in almost every way a remarkable contrast to that of his predecessor, Bishop Aquablanca. It is said that the Bishop of Worcester, his great-uncle, asked him as a child as to his choice of a profession, and that he answered he would like to be a soldier. "Then, sweetheart," his uncle is said to have exclaimed, "thou shalt be a soldier to serve the King of Kings, and fight under the banner of the glorious martyr, St. Thomas." Regular attendance at mass was his custom from earliest years. Both at Oxford and Paris he distinguished himself, gaining his degree of M.A. at the Sorbonne, and on his return accepted, at the request of the university of Oxford and with the consent of the King, the office of chancellor. In this capacity he showed singular courage and determination in repressing a brawl between the southern scholars and those of the north, in which we are told he escaped with a whole skin, but not with a whole coat.

He was chosen to fill the post of Chancellor of England under Simon de Montfort, at whose death, however, he was deprived of the office. It was some years after this that he became Bishop of Hereford, and was consecrated at Canterbury, September 8th, 1275. No Welsh bishop attended the consecration.

After he became a bishop he still wore his hair-shirt and showed ever intense devotion in his celebration of divine service. He was remarkable in the steadfastness and ability he displayed in maintaining the rights of the see. Gilbert de Clare, Earl of Gloucester, claiming a certain "chace" near Malvern Forest, whence came the Bishop's supply of game, found a relentless opponent in Bishop Cantilupe. The Bishop was prepared with the customary "pugil" or champion (who received 6s. 8d. per annum), though his services were not required. The Earl was excommunicated, and appealing to the law in a trial Bishop Cantilupe eloquently maintained his right to capture "buck, doe, fawn, wild cat, hare, and all birds pertaining thereto," and as a result of the verdict being in his favour, caused a long trench to be dug on the crest of the Malvern Hills as a boundary line, which is still traceable.

Llewellyn, King of Wales, was made to restore three manors of which he had obtained unlawful possession; and Lord Clifford, for cattle-lifting and maltreating the Bishop's tenants, was compelled to walk barefoot to the high altar in the cathedral, while the Bishop personally chastised him with a rod.

Many cases did he fight out successfully, but his greatest struggle was on a question of testamentary jurisdiction with Peckham, Archbishop of Canterbury, by whom he was ultimately excommunicated and obliged to leave the country, attended by Swinfield, his faithful chaplain.

He obtained a decree in his favour from Pope Martin IV., but died on the homeward journey on August 25th, 1282.

THE HISTORY OF THE BUILDING.

He was buried in the church of St. Severus, near Florence; but his bones having been divided from the flesh by boiling, were later carried to England and solemnly placed in the Lady Chapel of the cathedral. It is said that the Earl of Gloucester, with whom Bishop Cantilupe had had the dispute about the chace, attended the ceremony, and that blood began to flow from the bones when he approached the casket containing them; upon which the Earl immediately restored the property he had taken unjustly from the church.

Forty years later Bishop Cantilupe was canonised. It is said, amongst other evidences of his saintliness, that he never allowed his sister to kiss him. Three hundred sick people are said to have been cured at the place of his interment, and so many candles were presented by the crowds of visitors that Luke de Bray, the treasurer of the cathedral, had a dispute with the prebendaries as to the value of the wax, two-thirds being finally assigned to the treasurer and one-third to the prebendaries.

After five years Bishop Cantilupe's bones were removed to the Chapel of St. Katherine, in the north-west transept, on Maundy Thursday, April 6th, 1287, in presence of King Edward I. They were again twice moved in the sixteenth century to the Lady Chapel and back again to the north-west transept.

The building of the chapter-house may have spread over some part of Cantilupe's episcopate, and probably part of the cloisters were erected about this time.

The miracles said to have been wrought at the shrine of St. Cantilupe are both many and various. More than sixty-six dead people are said to have been restored to life. The saint's intervention appears to have been extended even to animals, as we find that King Edward I. twice sent sick falcons to be cured at this tomb. So great was the reverence for the saint that the See of Hereford was allowed by the Crown to change its armorial bearings for the arms of Cantilupe, which all its bishops have since borne.

Bishop Cantilupe was succeeded by his devoted chaplain, Richard Swinfield, an excellent preacher and a man of agreeable manners. Bishop Swinfield, like his predecessor, stoutly vindicated the rights and discipline of his diocese, once against a layman for taking forcible possession of a vacant benefice, another time against a lady for imprisoning a young clergyman in her castle on a false charge, and also against the people of Ludlow for violating the right of sanctuary, and in many cases against abuses of all sorts. On one occasion Pontius de Cors, a nephew of Bishop Aquablanca, who had obtained from the Pope the provision of the prebend of Hinton, interrupted the installation of Robert de Shelving appointed by Bishop Swinfield, gained admission to the cathedral with an accomplice, and was formally installed by him in spite of the remonstrance of the Chapter. He held his place by force of arms during that day and the next, but later submitted to the Bishop.

Bishop Swinfield was probably the builder of the nave-aisles and of the two easternmost transepts. This amounted to a remodelling of the work of De Vere. The bases of his piers and responds were retained and may still be seen, and upon the former octagonal columns were erected to carry the vaulting. The windows were altered throughout. It was in his time that the "*Mappa Mundi*," the curious map of the world designed by Richard of Haldingham of Battle in Sussex, a prebendary of Hereford in 1305, now preserved in the cathedral, came into possession of the Chapter.

Richard Haldingham was a great friend of Bishop Swinfield, and when it was necessary for him to send representatives to a provincial Council in London, A.D. 1313, Haldingham was deputed to attend with Adam of Orleton, a place belonging to the Mortimers of Wigmore in the north-east of Herefordshire.

Three years later (1316), on the death of Bishop Swinfield at his chief residence, Bosbury, Adam of Orleton succeeded him in the bishopric.

King Edward II. was not jubilant over the appointment of a friend of Roger Mortimer to this important position, and, failing to persuade Adam to decline the bishopric, he appealed to the Pope, begging him to cancel the appointment, but with no more success. The fortunes of the Bishop of Hereford became identified with the Queen, whom he joined on her return from France with her eldest son. It was at Hereford that this youth, then fourteen years of age, was appointed guardian of the kingdom under the direction of his mother.

The King, who had sought refuge in Wales, was captured at Neath Abbey, and the great seal taken from him by Bishop Adam Orleton, while the Chancellor, Hugh Despenser, was con-

THE HISTORY OF THE BUILDING. 13

veyed to Hereford, where he was crowned with nettles and dressed in a shirt upon which was written passages from Psalm lii. beginning, "Why boastest thou thyself, thou tyrant: that thou canst do mischief." Amid the howlings of a great multitude who mocked his name by shrieking "Hue!" he was finally hanged on a gallows 50 feet high and then quartered. Among the prisoners were two wearing holy orders, and these the Bishop of Hereford claimed as his perquisite.

A GARGOYLE IN THE CLOISTERS.   DRAWN BY A. HUGH FISHER.

Bishop Adam, wary, unscrupulous, but at the same time vigorous and of unusual ability, played a great part in politics to the end of the wretched King's life. Some historians still believe that he recommended the murder; he certainly supported the deposition in Parliament, and went to Kenilworth as one of the commissioners to force the King's resignation. If thus interested in secular politics, he was no less watchful and vigilant in the affairs of his bishopric and the cathedral.

The great central tower, destined centuries later to be a source of such anxiety and a problem of such difficulty to the restorer, was even at this early date showing signs of dilapidation, and Bishop Orleton obtained from Pope John XXII. a grant of the great tithes of Shenyngfeld (Swinfield) and Swalefeld (Swallowfield) in Berkshire, in answer to the following petition :—"That they, being desirous of rebuilding a portion of the fabric of the Church of Hereford, had caused much superstructure of sumptuous work to be built, to the adornment of the House of God, upon an ancient foundation; which in the judgment of masons or architects, who were considered skilful in their art, was thought to be firm and sound, at the cost of 20,000 marcs sterling and more, and that on account of the weakness of the aforesaid foundation, the building, which was placed upon it now, threatened such ruin, that by a similar judgment no other remedy could be applied short of an entire renovation of the fabric from the foundation,—which, on account of the expenses incurred in prosecution of the canonisation of Thomas de Cantilupe, Bishop of Hereford, of blessed memory, they were unable to undertake." The "sumptuous work" alluded to was evidently the central tower and the north transept; which latter had been built, as mentioned before, for the remains and shrine of Bishop Cantilupe.

When Mr. R. Biddulph Phillips, some sixty years ago, was examining the confused and unsorted mass of charters and grants in the possession of the cathedral, he found a parchment (which bore the two beautiful episcopal seals of Bishop Roger le Poer of Sarum and Bishop Adam de Orleton of Hereford) that acknowledged and confirmed this grant of tithes to the sustentation of the fabric of the cathedral, which still forms the backbone of the fabric fund. In 1328 Bishop Orleton was translated to Worcester.

During the ensuing war with France, the church walls echoed with prayers for the King's success, and, while the war-cloud still darkened the political sky, orisons louder and more heartfelt filled the cathedral. It is said that when the "Black Death" reached Hereford in 1349, to retard its progress in the city the shrine of St. Thomas de Cantilupe was carried in procession.

About this time, and possibly not unconnected with the calamity of this terrible plague, Bishop Trilleck issued a mandate prohibiting the performance of "theatrical plays and interludes" in churches as "contrary to the practice of religion." The exact character of these performances is doubtful, and the prohibition may have referred to some kind of secular mumming. The mystery play survived long after Bishop Trilleck's time in an annual pageant exhibited in the cathedral on Corpus Christi Day, to assist in which some of the city guilds were obliged by the rules of their incorporation.

The quarrels between the townspeople and the Bishop about his rights of jurisdiction continued with more or less frequency. It must certainly have been irritating to good Bishop Trilleck "*gratus, prudens, pius,*" as the mutilated inscription on his effigy describes him, when one William Corbet forced his way into the palace, carried away the porter bodily, shut him in the city gaol, and took away the keys of the palace.

On the second visitation of the "Black Death," 1361–2, it is said that the city market was removed from Hereford to a place about a mile on the west of the town, still marked by a cross called the "White Cross" bearing the arms of Bishop Charleton.

If Bishop Orleton was deeply concerned in the deposition of King Edward II., a later Bishop of Hereford, Thomas Trevenant, who was appointed in 1389 by papal provision, was no less active in the deposition of King Richard II., and was sent to the Pope with the Archbishop of York by Henry IV. to explain his title to the Crown and announce his accession.

In 1396, during the episcopate of Bishop Gilbert, the priest vicars of the cathedral were formed into a college by Royal Charter, and the first warden or "*custos*" was appointed by the King to show that the right of appointment was vested in the Crown. The college was to have a common seal, and to exercise the right of acquiring and holding property, but to be subject to the Dean and Chapter of the cathedral. Its members were the priests of the chantry chapels in the cathedral, at this time apparently twenty-seven in number.

In 1475 the college was moved from Castle Street to its present site, so that the vicars should be able more comfortably to attend the night services. An order was also made about this time concerning the celebration of mass at the altar of St. John Baptist in the cathedral, an arrangement which shows that then as now the parish of St. John had no church of its own outside the cathedral walls.

About 1418, the cloister connecting the Bishop's palace with the cathedral was begun by Bishop Lacy, who took great interest in the cathedral although he never visited his diocese. It was upon this work of the cloisters that 2800 marks were expended by Bishop Spofford, 1421-1448, in whose time the great west window was erected by William Lochard, the precentor. The richly panelled and vaulted chapel of Bishop Stanbury, approached from the north aisle of the presbytery, was added between 1453 and 1474.

In 1492 Edmund Audley, the Bishop of Rochester, was translated to Hereford, and during his episcopate founded the two-storied chantry chapel south of the Lady Chapel and near the shrine of St. Thomas of Cantilupe. The upper story was probably intended as a private oratory for the Bishop himself. Bishop Audley also presented to the cathedral a silver shrine.

THE AUDLEY CHAPEL.

The next important alteration was the lengthening of the great north porch which bears the date 1519 and the shields of Bishop Booth and his predecessor, Bishop Mayo. It is a very fine piece of Perpendicular work, somewhat similar in design to the porch in the middle of the west front of Peterborough Cathedral. At his death Bishop Booth left various books to the cathedral library and some tapestry for the high altar, together with silver and gold ornaments for the Cantilupe Shrine. The tapestry displayed the story of David and Nabal. He also bequeathed, amongst other things to his successor, the gold ring with which he was consecrated, but notwithstanding his forethought in specifying that these articles were not to be taken away with such successor in case of his translation, they have disappeared. Little could Bishop Booth have imagined, in the enthusiasm of his building operations, the changes to follow so closely upon his death. Yet the papal supremacy had been abolished in this country in 1534, and though the church services remained unaltered, the amended Primer had been published. On September 26th, 1535, was consecrated at Winchester, to the See of Hereford, one of the most "excellent instruments" of the Reformation, Edward Foxe, and in the following year the suppression of the monasteries began in serious earnest. Still the chantry chapels were to be spared for some time. Of these chantries and chapels there were then no less than twenty-one in the cathedral.

In 1553, commissioners were appointed to visit the churches, chapels, guilds, and fraternities all over the kingdom and take inventories of their treasures, leaving to each parish church or chapel "one or two chalices according to the multitude of people." In Hereford Cathedral, amongst other valuable ornaments, was a chalice of gold weighing 22 lbs. 9½ oz., two basins weighing 102 oz., and an enamelled pastoral staff in five pieces of silver gilt weighing 11 lbs. 7 oz. 3 dwts. troy. It is not possible to learn the value of the goods appropriated in the cathedral alone, but the jewels and plate of the whole country were estimated at 4860¼ ounces, in value about £1213, 1s. 3d.

On August 22nd or 25th, 1642, the Royal Standard was set up at Nottingham, and the clouds of the Great Rebellion burst over the country. Bishop Coke of Hereford had been one of the twelve churchmen most active against the Bill for excluding the bishops from Parliament, passed in the Commons in May 1641, and was one of the ten bishops committed to the Tower by the joint sentence of the Lords and Commons on charge of treason.

The "popishly inclined" county of Hereford was at one with its Bishop, but so unprepared for war that Lord Stamford, with two troops of cavalry and a single infantry regiment, entered Hereford under the orders of the Earl of Essex and quartered himself in the Bishop's palace. Here he remained till December 14th without, however, any serious plundering in the town itself. In April 1643, Waller took the city for the second time, and again without much resistance, a condition of the surrender being the immunity of the Bishop and cathedral clergy from personal violence and plunder. On his leaving Hereford the place was retaken by the Royalists, and became an asylum for fugitive Roman Catholics. So it went on, being held first by one side and then by the other. In the autumn of 1645 Hereford was besieged by Lord Leven with the Scottish army, who were driven off by Colonel Barnabas Scudamore with heavy loss.

The cathedral at this time suffered considerable injury during the siege. The defenders used the lead from the chapter-house roof to cover the keep of the castle, and possibly also to make bullets. Finally, on December 18th, through the treachery of Colonel Birch, the governor of the city, Hereford was once more taken, and this time the whole place was overrun by a rabble of plundering soldiery.

No doubt much damage had been done in the cathedral during the Reformation, but despite the protests of an antiquarian captain, one Silas Taylor, far greater mischief was perpetrated in this military loot. "The storied windows richly dight" were smashed to bits, monumental brasses torn up, the library plundered of most valuable MSS., and rich ornaments stolen.

Some while after the Restoration, an appeal was made by the cathedral clergy to the nobility, baronets, knights, esquires, and gentry of the county for help towards restoring the cathedral, though it is not known with what welcome the appeal was received.

Towards the beginning of the eighteenth century much harm was done to the cathedral by the zeal of Bishop Bisse, one of those irritating people who mean well but act abominably. He spent much, both on the palace and the cathedral, employing in the alterations of the former the stones of the chapter-house, which had been doubtless much injured but not irreparably so. In the cathedral itself he erected a mass of masonry intended to support the central tower, which was, however, nothing but a hideous architectural blunder. In itself it was ugly to behold, and actually weakened by lateral pressure that which it was intended to support. He also presented an elaborate altar-piece and Grecian oak screen with scenic decoration above, boards painted to represent curtains, and wooden imitations of tassels which hung immediately over the heads of the ministering priests as they stood at the altar. These were found later on to be hung on rusty nails by twine "little better than pack thread."

During the episcopate of the Hon. Henry Egerton, 1723-1746, an ancient building of early Norman date used as a chapel for the palace was pulled down. It consisted of an upper and a lower portion, the lower a chapel dedicated to St. Katherine and the upper one to St. Mary Magdalene. Part of one wall still remains. It was during the next episcopate, on Easter Monday 1786, that a terrible calamity occurred,—the fall of the great western tower. Directly and indirectly this was

THE WEST FRONT (FROM AN OLD PRINT).

the worst accident that has happened to Hereford Cathedral. The west front was utterly destroyed, and a great part of the nave seriously injured, while the injudicious restoration begun in 1788 by the Dean and Chapter, with James Wyatt for architect, did nearly as much to ruin the cathedral as the fall of the tower.

Already, at Salisbury, Wyatt had been busy with irreparable

[*From a drawing by T. Hearne, 1806.*]

THE NAVE AFTER THE FALL OF THE WEST END.

deeds of vandalism, but at Hereford he surpassed his previous efforts in this direction. He altered the whole proportion of the building, shortening the nave by a bay of 15 feet, erected a new west front on a "neat Gothic pattern," and availed himself of the chance of removing all the Norman work in the nave, above the nave arcade substituting a design of his own.

One of the strangest items in his scheme was a plaster hod moulding round each of the arches above the arcade. These eccentricities were removed not long since, but the roughened lines for adhesion of the plaster still remain. Inside the west front may also still be seen large spaces of wall painted to represent blocks of stone, but no more so in reality than the wall of any stucco residence.

It should not be forgotten, while condemning the meaningless insipidity of Wyatt's work, that it was enthusiastically approved in his own day, and that the public generally were as much to blame as himself.

The old spire was taken down from the central tower, and in order to give it apparent height the roofs of both nave and choir were lowered in pitch, its parapet was raised, and some pinnacles were added.

At the same time the churchyard was levelled and new burying-grounds provided for the city elsewhere.

In 1837, Dr. Thomas Musgrave was promoted to the See of Hereford. He was a man of sound judgment and of much practical ability, and it was during his episcopacy that a serious competent and thorough repair of the cathedral was at last undertaken at a cost of £27,000, to which no one devoted more loving care or more untiring energy than Dean Merewether.

"Is it time for you, O ye, to dwell in your ceiled houses and this house lie waste?" he quotes in the beginning of his exhaustive "Statement of the condition and circumstances of the Cathedral Church of Hereford in the year 1841." In this statement he shows the lamentable state of decay in the eastern end of the Lady Chapel, the bulging of its walls and the dangerous fissures, which, on the removal of whitewash and plaster, became visible in the soffit of each of the window arches.

In early times the walls were very much thicker, composed of hewn stone, making a kind of casing at each side, called ashlar, the interval being filled with rubble masonry cemented with lime and loam. This stuffing having deteriorated the weight above had split the outer wall, though most fortunately the interior face was perfectly sound and upright.

To trace the cracks thoroughly, it was necessary to remove the oak panelling fitted to the wall below the windows, and the heavy bookcases filling up a great part of the area were taken away with the lath and plaster partition from the sides of the pillar at the west end of the chapel.

THE CATHEDRAL FROM THE NORTH AT THE END OF THE SEVENTEENTH CENTURY.

By this clearing the beauty of the chapel so long obscured became again manifest: its symmetrical proportions, the remains of its ancient painting, the disclosure of two most interesting monuments, two aumbries, a double piscina, the chapel of Bishop Audley, but more important than all, two of the most beautiful specimens of transition arches to be found anywhere, Early English in form, but ornamented in their soffits with the Norman moulding and the zigzag decoration, corresponding with the remarkable union of the Norman intersecting arches on the exterior of the building, with its pointed characteristics.

The further examination by Dean Merewether and Mr. Cottingham, the architect, showed that the great central tower of the cathedral was in imminent danger of falling, and might at any moment entirely collapse.

Above the Grecian altar screen of Bishop Bisse they were struck by the traces of Norman mouldings, whilst on traversing the clerestory gallery the remains of Norman ornaments were everywhere to be found, the gallery itself being still existent at each side, returned behind the wooden coverings, up to the splays of the eastern windows.

The whole incongruous covering of the east end of the choir shown on p. 77 was then removed, and the change effected was most striking. It was evident that long before the introduction of the Grecian screen in 1717, the original arrangement had been disturbed by the insertion of a Perpendicular window, to support which the low circular arch in the centre had been constructed; on either side of this window were now to be seen the mouldings and featherings of the original early decorated lights, on a level with the lateral clerestory range; below these the Norman arcade, based upon a string course of nebule ornaments.

"But below," says Dean Merewether, "the beauty of beauties was to be traced,—the thickness of that part of the wall is 8 feet; on either side of the arch, 24 feet in span, were portions of shafts, corresponding with the pair of Norman shafts exposed to view seven years ago. The bases of these (standing on a sort of plinth, which was continued through those already referred to), as well as the capitals, of most curious detail, were perfect, and upon them were visible as far as the level of the window above, the remaining stones which formed the architecture of the exterior arch, from which it was evident that its crown must have risen to the height of 30 feet. By cautious examination of the parts walled up, it was discovered that the capitals were all perfect, and that this exquisite and grand construction, the mutilation and concealment of which it is utterly impossible to account for, was, in fact, made up of five arches, the interior and smallest supported by the two semi-columns already described, and each of the others increasing in span as it approached the front upon square and circular shafts alternately, the faces of each arch being beautifully decorated with the choicest Norman ornaments. Of the four lateral arches, the two first had been not only hidden by the oak panelling of the screen, but were also, like the two others, closed up with lath and plaster, as the central arch; and when these incumbrances and desecrations were taken away, it is impossible to describe adequately the glorious effect produced, rendered more solemn and impressive by the appearance of the ancient monuments of Bishops Reynelm, Mayew, Stanbury, and Benet, whose ashes rest beneath these massive arches, of which, together with the noble triforium above, before the Conquest, Athelstan had probably been the founder, and the former of those just mentioned, the completer and restorer after that era."

Under Mr. Cottingham many improvements were made, though it cannot be said that all the work he did was good either in design or execution. The beautiful lantern of the central tower, with its fifty-six shafts, was satisfactorily strengthened and thrown open to view. At the time of Dean Merewether's death in 1850 much still remained to be done, and in 1857 a further scheme was set going under the financial management of Dean Richard Dawes, and the architectural direction of Mr., afterwards Sir Gilbert, Scott, who restored the north transepts, the north porch, the choir, and Lady Chapel. He also erected the large metal screen and fitted up the Lady Chapel as a church for the parish of St. John the Baptist.

Altogether in these two works of repair about £45,000 was expended, and the cathedral was opened for service on June 30th, 1863.

CHAPTER II.

THE CATHEDRAL—EXTERIOR.

ARTISTIC unity is certainly not the chief characteristic of Hereford Cathedral, but it is doubtful whether the absence of that quality dear to a purist is not more than compensated for by the fine examples of different periods, which make the massive pile as a whole a valuable record of historical progress. And surely it is more fitting that a great ecclesiastical edifice should grow with the successive ages it outlasts, and bear about it architectural evidence of every epoch through which it has passed.

Almost in the midst of the city the sturdy mass of the cathedral building reposes in a secluded close, from which the best general view is obtained. The close is entered either from Broad Street, near the west window, or from Castle Street; the whole of the building lying on the south side of the close between the path and the river. The space between the Wye and the cathedral is filled by the Bishop's Palace and the college of the Vicars Choral.

On the east are the foundations of the castle, which was formerly one of the strongest on the Welsh marches.

The cathedral is especially rich in architecture of the Norman, Early English, and Early Decorated periods.

The work of the Norman builders, found chiefly in the interior, survives in the exterior aspect rather in the "sturdy" quality remaining through the subsequent building being imposed upon the old foundations. The side apses of the original triple eastern termination were converted into the present eastern transept; an operation, the result of which helps to produce an intricate outline already irregular through the projections of the porch of Bishop Booth.

THE CATHEDRAL—EXTERIOR. 27

The **Central Tower**, a splendid example of Decorated work, is of two stages above the roofs, with buttresses at the angles. It is covered with a profusion of ball-flower ornament,

Photochrom Co., Ld., Photo.]

BISHOP BOOTH'S PORCH AND NORTH TRANSEPT.

which, except in the south nave aisle of Gloucester Cathedral, is nowhere else so freely used.

Pershore Abbey is not far from Hereford, and from the disposition of the upper windows of the central tower and the style and position of the dividing pilasters and bands of ornament, it seems likely that the earlier lantern of Pershore is partly responsible for its design.

In old prints of the cathedral the great central spire which formerly existed is shown. It was a timber erection, covered with lead. When this was taken down at the time of the great repairs and rebuilding of the west end, a stunted, squat appearance was given to the building. In the year 1830 Canon Russell presented a sum of money to the Dean and Chapter to build four appropriate pinnacles at the angles.

The tower which formerly stood at the west end was similar in design to the central one, but rose only one stage above the leads of the nave. This seems to have been used as a belfry; whereas the central tower was a lantern.

The large projecting **North Porch**, completed in 1530 by Bishop Booth, is Perpendicular, and somewhat resembles, though it is later in date, the porch in the centre of the west front at Peterborough. The front entrance archway has highly enriched spandrels and two lateral octagonal staircase buttress turrets at the angles. These have glazed windows in the upper portions, forming a picturesque lantern to each. This outer porch consists of two stories, the lower of which is formed by three wide, open arches, springing from four piers at the extreme angles, two of which are united with the staircase turrets, the others with the ends of the old porch. The upper story, containing an apartment, is sustained on a vaulted and groined roof, and has three large windows, with elaborate tracery.

In the north transept the massive buttresses with bevelled angles, of which those at the angles are turreted, with spiral cappings, the remarkable windows, tall without transoms, and rising nearly the whole height of the building, show to great advantage. The clerestory windows, like those in the outer wall of the triforium in the nave of Westminster, are triangular on the exterior.

On the eastern side of this transept, which has an aisle, is an unusual architectural feature. The windows of the triforium have semi-circular arched mouldings, enclosing a window of three lights of lancet-shaped arches. Beneath the aisle window is a pointed arched doorway, which was probably an original approach to the shrine of Cantilupe.

In the angle is a staircase turret, which is circular at the bottom and polygonal above ; and this probably was an access to a private apartment for a monk over the aisle of the transept containing the sacred shrine.

Continuing an examination of the north side of the cathedral one notices the buttresses of the north-east transept, the Stanbury Chapel, the windows, parapet, and roof of the aisle, the clerestory windows with arcade dressings to the walls, and the modern parapet above the whole.

Photochrom Co., Ld., Photo.]

GENERAL VIEW, FROM THE WEST.

The style of the arcade and window, and also the blank window or double arch, with two smaller arches within the clerestory wall, claims especial attention, as well as the ribbed roof rising above the Norman triforium.

We now come to the Early English work of the **Lady Chapel**, the east end of which is especially noticeable, with its bold angular buttresses rising from immense bases. The numerous and large base mouldings running round the wall of this building, its tall lancet-shaped windows, arcades, and ovolar and lozenge-shaped panels, are so many interesting peculiarities of design.

The Audley Chapel projects on the south side. The angular, embattled parapet at the end is a modern addition.

The south side of the cathedral is not easily examined by the public, being shut within the walls of a garden between the Bishop's and the Vicars' Cloisters.

The **Bishop's Cloisters** consist of two walks only, or covered corridors, though that on the west, which was pulled down in the reign of Edward VI. to make room for a pile of brick building appropriated to the Grammar School, and in its turn demolished in 1836, is now in course of restoration.

It does not appear that the cloisters ever had a walk on the north side against the cathedral.

These cloisters are of Perpendicular date, and between a continued series of buttresses are windows of large dimensions, with mullions and tracery.

The vaulting of the roof is adorned with numerous ribbed mouldings, at the intersections of which are shields charged with sculptured figures, foliage, arms, etc. These ribs spring from slender pillars between the windows and corbels heads on the other side: over the exterior of the windows are carved grotesque heads, of which we give some illustrations. The south walk of the cloisters is the more richly groined. At the south-east corner is a square turreted tower containing a small chamber, which has been carefully and completely restored. It has always been called the "Ladye Arbour," although no one has been able to discover the origin of this name or the use to which the chamber was put; many antiquarians suggest a possible reference to the Virgin.

The entrance doorway to the **Chapter-house** from the east walk still remains, but is walled up. It consists of a pointed arch under a lofty, richly ornamented pedimental moulding, having clustered shafts on the sides, with foliated capitals. The archway is divided by a slender pillar into two smaller openings. The once elegant chapter-room to which this doorway communicated, whether or not they fell, as Britton asserts, "beneath the fanatic frenzy of the Cromwellian soldiers," was certainly neglected; and then, as long as any material could be got from it, treated as a stone quarry by Bishop Bisse and his successors. This chapter-house appears to have been a beautiful piece of design of the rich Decorated period. It was decagonal in plan, with a projecting buttress

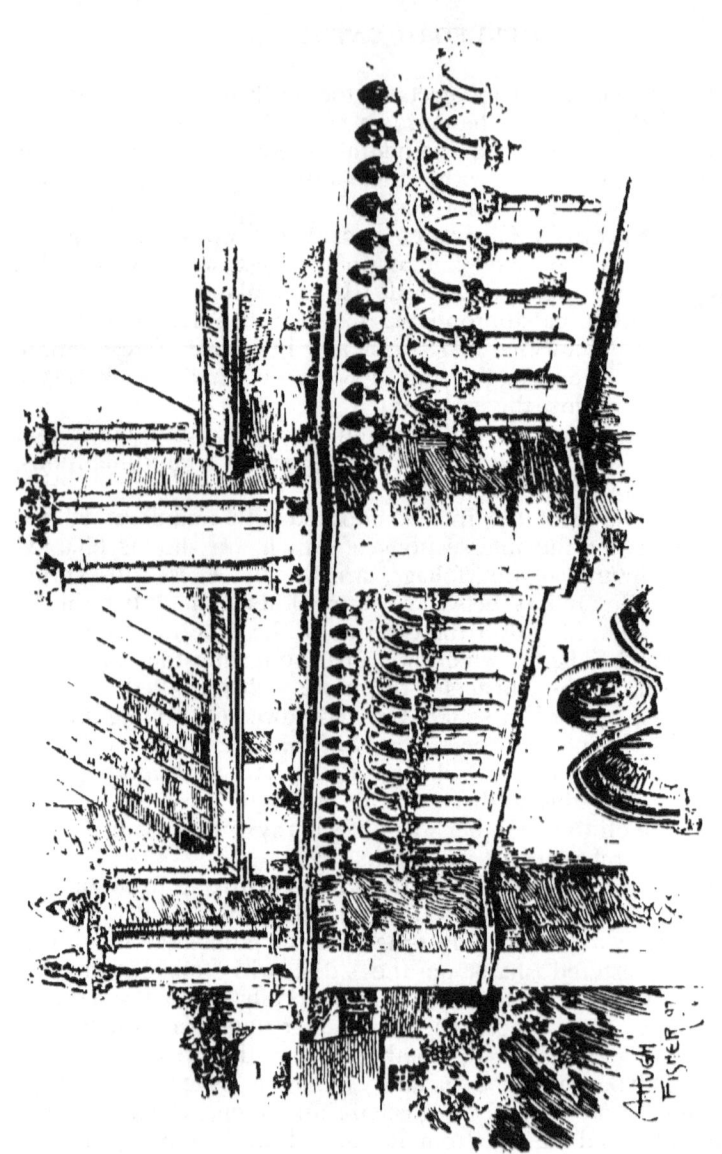

EXTERIOR OF THE LADY CHAPEL. DRAWN BY A. HUGH FISHER

at each angle. Each side, except the one occupied by the entrance, was sub-divided into five panels or seats. Remains of three sides only are left, and these only as far as the window-sills.

Against the south wall of the cloisters, towards its east end, are some remains of two Norman chapels, one above the other. The lower was dedicated to St. Katherine and the upper to St. Mary Magdalene.

"The form, excepting a portico and choir (*i.e.* chancel) was an exact square; four pillars in the middle, with arches every way, supported the roof; the portico was composed of a succession of arches retiring inwards, and had a grandeur in imitation of Roman works: two pillars on each side consisted of single stones. There was a descent of a few steps to the lower chapel, which had several pillars against the walls made of single stones, and an octagonal cupola on the four middle pillars. The walls were much painted, and the arched roof was turned with great skill, and resembled the architecture which prevailed during the declension of the Roman Empire" (see Stukeley, Havergal, etc.).

Mentioning the existence of the doorway and two small windows in the remaining north wall, the author of *The Picturesque Antiquities of Hereford* proceeds to say: "These are extremely interesting, as they pertained to an edifice which once stood on the south side of this wall, and is believed to have been the original church of St. Mary, the patron saint of the cathedral before the translation of the body of St. Ethelbert. It was the parish church of St. Mary, to which the residences in the cathedral close belonged. Transcripts of registers of marriages there solemnised so late as the year 1730 are existent in the Dean's archives."

A second cloister, known as the **Vicars' Cloister**, connects the Vicars' College with the south-east transept. The arrangement here may be compared with that of Chichester, as showing the most probable plan of the latter before the destruction of the south walk and its connection with the cloister of the Vicars Choral.

In the area of the Bishop's Cloister was formerly a preaching cross, which fell into a decayed state during the latter part of the last century. Beneath it was a dome of masonry which closed the aperture to a well of considerable depth, which had been formed with great exactness. This well still exists beneath a plain square stone. Another well was (according to Stukeley) situated between the College and the Castle Green, with a handsome stone arch over it.

Photochrom Co., Ld., Photo.]
THE CLOISTERS, WITH THE LADIES' ARBOUR.

Building operations are still in progress at Hereford, and it was proposed to mark the year of Her Majesty's Jubilee by a special restoration, dealing principally with the west end and central tower.

CHAPTER III.

THE INTERIOR OF THE CATHEDRAL.

The Cathedral is usually entered from the north-west through the beautiful parvise porch of Bishop Booth. The lower stage of this porch is formed by three arches with octagonal turrets at their outer angles. These turrets are each capped by a lantern. The second stage has three fine Perpendicular windows. The doorway, which actually opens into the church, belongs to a smaller porch within this outer one. The inner porch is of the Decorated period. There is some particularly good iron-work on the doors, made by Messrs Potter from designs by Mr. Cottingham, junior.

Hereford has a smaller area than either of the other two sister cathedrals, being only 26,850 feet in extent.

The **Nave**, which is separated from the aisles by eight massive Norman piers (part of the original church), of which the capitals are worthy of notice, has somewhat suffered by restorations at the hand of Wyatt. The triforium, the clerestory, the vaulting of the roof and the western wall and doorway are all his work; and it must not be forgotten that he shortened the original nave by one entire bay. Walking to the west end, from which the best general view is to be obtained, one is impressed by the striking effect of the great Norman piers and arches and the gloom of the choir beyond. Through the noble circular arches, which support the central tower and the modern screen on the eastern side of it, we see the eastern wall of the choir, pierced above by three lancet windows and below by a wide circular arch receding in many orders. A central pillar divides this lower arch, two pointed arches springing from its capital and leaving a spandrel between them, which is covered with modern sculpture. In the far distance

THE NORTH PORCH.

may be distinguished the east wall of the Lady Chapel and its brilliant lancet lights.

Throughout the Cathedral the Norman work is remarkable for the richness of its ornament as compared with other buildings of the same date, such as Peterborough or Ely.

The main arches of the nave are ornamented with the billet and other beautiful mouldings, and the capitals of both piers and shafts are also elaborately decorated. The double half shafts set against the north and south fronts of the huge circular piers are in the greater part restorations.

Over each pier arch there are two triforium arches imitated from the Early English of Salisbury. They are divided by slender pillars, but there is no triforium passage.

During the Late Decorated period the nave-aisles were practically rebuilt, the existing walls and windows being erected upon the bases of the Norman walls, which were retained for a few feet above the foundations. The vaulting of the roofs of the nave-aisles and the roof of the nave itself were coloured under the direction of Mr. Cottingham.

The Font, of late Norman design, probably twelfth century, is in the second bay of the south aisle beginning from the west.

The circular basin is 32 inches in diameter, large enough for the total immersion of children. Beneath arches round the basin are figures of the twelve Apostles. These, however, with one exception, have been much broken. The most curious feature of this interesting font is the base with four demi-griffins or lions projecting therefrom. The whole is protected by a mosaic platform.

Monuments in the Nave.—The first monument on the south side as we walk from the western end is the fine effigy in alabaster of Sir Richard Pembridge in plate and mail armour with his greyhound. This monument was formerly at the Black Friars Monastery, but was removed here at the Suppression. Sir Richard Pembridge was a Knight of the Garter (53rd of that order) at the time of Edward III., and was present at Poitiers. He died in 1375. There are still traces of colour on this monument and gold remains on the points of the cap to which the camail is fastened, as also on the jewelled sword-belt. A sheaf of green coloured feathers is separated from the tilting helmet, on which the head rests, by a coronet of open roses. When the effigy was brought here it had but one leg

THE INTERIOR OF THE CATHEDRAL.   37

left, and that the gartered one. A wooden limb was carved, and the workman showed such accuracy in duplicating the stone leg that the Knight was adorned with a pair of garters for many years until Lord Saye and Sele, Canon Residentiary, presented the Cathedral with a new alabaster leg, and the wooden one was banished to a shelf in the library.

Under a foliated Decorated arch in the wall in the fifth bay

Photochrom Co., Ld., Photo.]
THE NAVE.

is the carved figure of an unknown ecclesiastic. The effigy is headless and otherwise much mutilated.

In the sixth bay is another mutilated and headless figure, under a foliated arch, which is crowned by a bearded head wearing a cap. It is thought to be the monument of a former treasurer.

In the fifth bay a quaint door leads from the aisle to the Bishop's Cloister. This has a square heading which rises above the sill of the window over it. There is an interesting series of heads in the hollow moulding, which are said to be copies of earlier work in the same position. The iron-work of the door itself is modern by Potter. A lofty Norman arch leads from this aisle into the south transept.

The north aisle of the nave is similar in style to the south. It contains six memorial windows to Canon Clutton and his wife, with subjects by Warrenton from the life of St. John the Baptist.

In the sixth bay from the west of the north wall of the nave is the effigy and tomb under which is buried Bishop Booth (1535), the builder of the large projecting porch which bears his name. The recumbent figure of the Bishop is fully vested with a *mitra pretiosa* with pendent fillets. He wears a cassock, amice, alb, stole, fringed tunic and dalmatic, and chasuble with orfrays in front. On his feet are broad-toed sandals; his hands are gloved; a crozier (the head of which has been broken) is veiled on the right. At this side is a feathered angel. The original inscription, cut into stone and fixed above the effigy, remains uninjured :

"Carolus Booth, episcopus Herefordensis cum 18 annos, 5 menses et totidem dies Ecclesiæ huic cum laude præfuisset, quinto die Maii 1535 defunctus sub hoc tumulo sepultus jacet."

The iron-work in front of this tomb is the only specimen in the Cathedral which has not been disturbed, although Mr. Havergal says "most of our large ancient monuments were protected by iron railings." It is divided into six square panels, having shields and heraldic ornaments.

The beautiful wrought iron **Screen,** an elaborate example of artistic metal-work, painted and gilt, executed by Messrs Skidmore of Coventry, from designs by Sir Gilbert Scott, stands between the eastern piers of the central tower, a little towards the nave. The first great piece of metal-work of this kind executed in England in modern times was the choir screen at Lichfield, designed and carried out by the same artists as the Hereford screen; though the latter and subsequent production transcends that of Lichfield, both in craftsmanship and beauty.

It has five main arches, each subdivided into two subarches by a slender shaft. The central arch is larger and higher than the others, is gabled and surmounted by a richly jewelled cross. This forms the entrance, and on either side, to a height of 4 feet, the lower part of the arches are filled with tracery in panels. The spandrels between the heads of the arches are enriched with elaborate ornament in flowing outline.

A variety of foliage and flowers has been worked in thin plates of copper and hammered iron, in imitation of natural specimens, and throughout the screen the passion flower is

THE CHOIR SCREEN.

prominent in the decoration. It is composed of 11,200 lbs. of iron, 5000 lbs. of copper and brass, 50,000 pieces of vitreous and other mineral substances in the mosaic panels, and about 300 cut and polished stones. There are also seven bronze figures, three single figures, and two groups. Of these the *Times*, May 29, 1862, well said: " These figures are perfect studies in themselves. Every one can understand them at a glance, and from the centre figure of Our Saviour to those of the praying Angels, the fulness of their meaning may be felt without the aid of any inscriptions beneath the feet to set forth who or what they are."

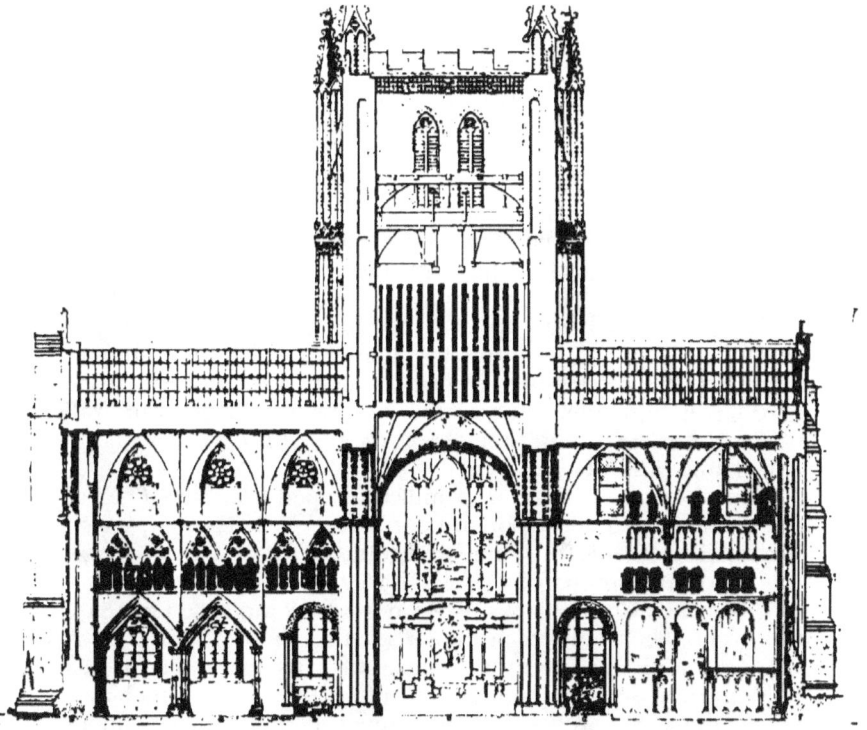

SECTION THROUGH TOWER AND TRANSEPTS.

The eastern side of the screen, though without statuary, is no less worthy of inspection. Over the gates the large oval space is filled with the sacred monogram I. H. C. The base consists of polished Devonshire marble. The diversity of tint of the metals used is in itself a source of colour, but the whole of the hammered iron-work of the foliage has been painted with oxides of iron and copper, while the colour scheme is further carried out in the mosaics.

The whole effect is certainly beautiful, and the screen is perhaps the best example of this kind of work produced in modern times. The cost of the screen was £3000, though the sum paid by the Chapter in accordance with their agreement was only £1500. The same firm, the Skidmore Art Company, who made it, also supplied the large corona and gasfittings.

A brass eagle presented by the Misses Rushort to the Cathedral, is placed near the south-west corner of the screen; it was designed by Cottingham.

The Central Tower.—Immediately above the four great arches of the central tower, the interior walls are, says Professor Willis in his report on the Cathedral, " Of a very singular construction; twelve piers of compact masonry on each side, beside angle piers, are carried up to the height of 26 ft., and connected half-way up by a horizontal course of stone, in long pieces, and by an iron bar, which runs all round immediately under this bonding course. Upon these gigantic stone gratings, if I may be allowed the expression, the interior wall of the tower rests, and they also carry the entire weight of the bell-chamber and bells.

The whole space is now completely open from the floor of the Cathedral to the wooden floor of the bell-chamber, which is painted underneath in blue and gold. From this floor hangs the handsome corona of wrought iron.

Before Mr. Cottingham's restoration was commenced in 1843, however, the whole appearance of the central tower was different, and the beautiful lantern with its many shafts was hidden from view by a vault of the fifteenth century, which rose above the great arches and completely concealed the upper portion of the tower.

In his specific report of the condition of the central tower in particular, which he was instructed to deliver in writing, Mr. Cottingham said:

"To enable me to form the opinion which I have now the honour of reporting, I have carefully examined the construction of the four great piers which support the tower; they are of Norman workmanship, and sufficient in bulk to carry a much greater weight than the present tower, had the masonry been more carefully constructed ; they consist of a series of semi-circular columns attached to a thin ashlar casing, which surrounds the piers, and the chambers or cavities within are filled with a rubble core, composed of broken stones, loam and lime grouting ; this was undoubtedly sufficient to carry a low Norman tower, but when the great Early English shaft was added on the top of this work the pressure became too great for such kind of masonry to bear. The ashlar and semi-columns, not being well bonded and deeply headed into the rubble cores, split and bulged, and the cores, for want of a proper proportion of lime, diminished and crushed to pieces. To remedy these defects, a second facing of ashlar has been attached to the piers, in some places by cutting out a part of the old ashlar, and in others by merely fixing long slips of stone round the pier with iron plugs, run in with lead,—these most unsightly excrescences have destroyed the beauty of the original design, without adding any strength to the masonry. The same unskilful hands blocked up all the original Norman arches, except one, connected with the tower piers and communicating with the aisles, choir, and transepts, leaving only a small passage-way in each.

"The first triforium arches in the choir and east side of the south transept, abutting against the tower, have also been closed up with masonry, so as to leave scarcely a trace of the rich work which lies concealed behind it. These injudicious performances have tended to weaken instead of strengthen the tower. The interior walls above the main arches of the tower, up to the bases of the fifty-two pillars, which surround the bell-ringers' chamber, are in a very ruinous state, particularly at the four angles, where rude cavities, running in a diagonal direction, have been made large enough for a man to creep in,—these unaccountable holes have tended very much to increase the danger, as all the masonry connected with them is drawn off its bond, and many of the stones shivered to pieces by the enormous pressure above. The stone-work, also, above the pillars, is drawn off at the angles just below the timber-work of the bell floor. On the whole, I never witnessed a more awful monument of the fallibility of human skill than the tower of Hereford Cathedral at this moment presents."

In addition to the report of the architect the Chapter availed themselves, on recommendation of the Bishop, of the opinion of Professor Willis, of Cambridge. This gentleman, after the most minute scrutiny and indefatigable labour, produced his elaborate and well-known report. He essentially corroborated the architect, especially as to the general state of the tower ; and, under the strenuous exertions of Dean Merewether, the great work of restoration was commenced. The tower contains a fine peal of ten bells in the key of C. A new clock was erected in 1861, which strikes the hours and quarter-hours.

The North Transept.
— Passing through the north arch of the tower we come into some of the most interesting parts of the Cathedral. The transept beyond was entirely rebuilt for the reception of the shrine of Bishop Cantilupe, when his body was removed from the Lady Chapel in 1287, after the miracles reported at his tomb had already largely increased the revenues of the Cathedral. The unusual shape of the arches and the fine and effective windows of this transept render it one of the most distinguished English specimens of the style.

On the north is a window with triple lights on each side of a group of banded shafts, the tracery above being formed of circles enclosing trefoils. The heads of the lights are sharply pointed.

NORTH ARCH OF CENTRAL TOWER, SHOWING MASONRY ERECTED ABOUT 1320.

The west side has two lofty windows recessed inside triangular-headed arches, which completely fill the two bays. They have three lights each, and are exactly similar to the windows on the north side of the transept.

Surrounded by alternate shafts of sandstone and dark

marble, a clustered pier divides the eastern aisle of the transept into two bays. These shafts have foliated capitals, and the bases have knots of foliage between them.

With the exception of one string of dog-tooth ornament the mouldings of the main arches are plain.

Above is the interesting triforium stretching across the Norman arch opening to the choir-aisle beyond the transept itself. There are in each bay two pointed arches, each containing three smaller arches with foiled headings surmounted by three open quatrefoils. The spandrels between the arches are diapered in low relief with leaf ornament. Above, far back in the clerestory arches, are octofoil windows with sills of overlapping courses, which incline forward to the string course above the triforium.

The shafts of all the windows are ringed at the angles, and the triangular arches are of an unusual stilted shape, similar to those in the clerestory of Worcester Cathedral on the south side of the nave. These are, however, of later date, and may have been imitated by the Worcester architect.

The restoration of the north transept by Sir G. G. Scott was satisfactorily carried out, and certainly improves the general effect.

Monuments in the North Transept.—The great north stained-glass window by Hardman was placed there as a memorial to Archdeacon Lane-Freer who died in 1863. Underneath this window, which is described later on in the section devoted to stained glass, is the stone effigy of Bishop Westfayling (died 1602). The canopy was removed by Wyatt, and the effigy is now leaning on its side against the wall. There is an undoubted original half-length portrait of this bishop in the Hall of Jesus College, Oxford. There are monuments to other members of the family in the church at Ross.

In the pavement near the choir-aisle is a brass to John Philips, the author of *The Splendid Shilling* and of *Cyder*, a poem endearing him to Herefordshire. His family belonged to this county, although he himself was born in Oxfordshire. There is also a monument to Philips in Poets' Corner, Westminster Abbey. He died in 1708, at the early age of 32.

The next monument in the north transept is the effigy of Bishop Thomas Charlton, treasurer of England, 1329. This

Photochrom Co. Ld., Photo.]

THE NORTH TRANSEPT.

effigy and its richly decorated alcove or canopy was most luckily not touched by Wyatt.

Here are stained-glass windows to Captain Arkwright, lost in an avalanche; Captain Kempson, and Rev. S. Clark, Headmaster of Battersea College.

In a line with the central pier of the eastern aisle is the most important monument in the north transept, viz.:—the pedestal of the celebrated shrine of St. Thomas de Cantilupe, 1282, who died at Civita Vecchia, near Florence, on his way to Rome, August 25th, 1282. His heart was sent to Ashridge in Buckinghamshire, part of the body was buried near Orvieto; and the bones were brought to Hereford and deposited in the Lady Chapel.

The pedestal is in shape a long parallelogram, narrower at the lower end. It is of Purbeck marble, and consists of two stages, the lower having a series of cinquefoiled niches and fourteen figures of Templars in chain armour in different attitudes, for Bishop Cantilupe was Provincial Grand Master of the Knights Templars in England.

All the figures are seated with various monsters under their feet. The filling of the spandrels between these niches and that of the spandrels between the arches of the upper stage is especially noteworthy. It belongs to the first Decorated period, and while the arrangement is still somewhat stiff or formal, the forms are evidently directly copied from nature.

The slab inside the open arcade, which forms the upper stage, still bears the matrix of the brass of an episcopal figure having traces of the arms of the See (*i.e.*, the arms of Cantilupe).

By the dedication of the north transept especially to Bishop Cantilupe was avoided the secondary part which his shrine must have played if it had been placed in the usual post of honour at the back of the high altar. The shrine of St. Ethelbert was probably already there, and wisely enough a distinguished position was specially created by rebuilding the north transept for the purpose. There is a similar state of affairs at Oxford Cathedral with the shrine of St. Frideswide, and in the south transept of Chichester Cathedral with that of St. Richard de la Wych.

We note also a brass to Dean Frowcester, 1529; and another to Richard Delamare and his wife Isabella (1435).

Near the Cantilupe shrine is a bust of Bishop Field (died

1636), and on the floor is an effigy of John D'Acquablanca, a Dean of Hereford (died 1320), and nephew of Bishop D'Acquablanca, whose beautiful monument is close to it, between the north choir-aisle and the eastern aisle of the transept. Beholding the exquisite grace of this tomb we are reminded of the more elaborate and equally beautiful chantry of the same period (1262) in the south choir transept of Salisbury to Bishop Giles de Bridport.

Over the effigy, which is a most interesting example of minute ecclesiastical costume, delicate shafts of Purbeck marble support a gabled canopy, each gable of which is surmounted by a finial in the form of a floriated cross.

This monument once glowed with rich colour, and in 186: a feeble attempt was made to restore it, which was, however, not carried out. Bishop Acquablanca, Peter of Savoy, had been steward of the household to his relative, William of Savoy, the Queen's uncle. His preferment was one of the noteworthy instances of Henry III.'s love of foreigners, and as Bishop of Hereford he was especially unpopular. The King made him his treasurer and consulted him on all matters of state. At his death, says the Rev. H. W. Phillott,[1] "He was probably little regretted in his cathedral city, whose citizens he had defeated in an attempt to encroach on his episcopal rights. But he used his victory with moderation, for he forgave them one half of their fine and devoted the other half to the fabric of the cathedral, probably that noble and graceful portion of it, the north-west transept, which contains the exquisitely beautiful shrine, probably erected by himself, under which repose the remains of his nephew, John, Dean of Hereford, as well as his own, his heart excepted, which, with a pathetic yearning of home-sickness, he desired should be carried to the church which he had founded in his own sunny land at Aigue-Belle, in Savoy. Yet, though his memory has received no mercy at the hands of historians and song-writers of his day, though his example did much to swell the tide of ill-repute in which many of the clergy of all ranks were held (for the laity, says the song-writer, are apt to pay less attention to the doctrine than to the life of their teachers), we ought not to leave out of sight that he did much to improve the fabric of the Cathedral, and bequeathed liberal gifts to its foundation in money, books,

[1] *The Diocese of Hereford*, H. W. Phillott.

THE CANTILUPE SHRINE.

ornaments, and land, and also a handsome legacy to the poor of the diocese."

In the north transept is a doorway leading to the tower.

South Transept.—Crossing the Cathedral in front of the Skidmore screen it is a relief to turn from the nave with its sham triforium to the south transept with its fine three stage Norman east side. The groining, although incongruous, is still beautiful, and does not irritate in the same way as Wyatt's abominations in the nave. This transept contains several disputed architectural points, and opinions are divided as to whether it may not be the oldest existing portion of the Cathedral. "At any rate," says G. Phillips Bevan,[1] "this transept seems to have been the happy hunting-ground of successive races of builders, who have left the side-walls in admired confusion."

Though it underwent great alteration in the Perpendicular period much of the Norman work remains. The east wall is in the best preservation, and is certainly entirely Norman with the exception of the groining. It is covered with five series of arcades, which may be divided into three stages. In the middle stage is a notably good triforium passage of very short Norman arches. All the other ranges of arcades, except those at the level of the clerestory, are blocked. On this side the transept is lighted from the clerestory by two Norman windows.

In both east and west walls there is a very fine Norman moulded double arch.

In the west wall Perpendicular windows have cut into the Norman work, and a large Perpendicular window nearly fills the south wall with panelling round it of the same period.

Monuments in the South Transept.—There is an interesting altar-tomb of Sir Alexander Denton, 1576, of Hillesden, Co. Bucks, Esq., and his lady and a child in swaddling clothes, toward the south-east angle of the transept. The effigies are in alabaster, and retain considerable traces of colour. They are in full proportion, and the knight wears a double chain and holds a cross in his hands. The Dentons were ancestors of the Coke family, now Earls of Leicester. The swaddled body of the child lies to the left of its mother,

[1] *Guide to the Wye and its Neighbourhood*, by the late G. Phillips Bevan, F.S.S.

its head resting on a little double pillow by her knee, and a part of the red cloth on which she lies wraps over the lower part of the babe.

To the right of the knight, balancing the child in the composition, lie his two gauntlets or mail gloves, which have been much scratched with names.

The head of the knight rests upon his helmet.

Round the verge of the tomb is this inscription:

"Here lieth Alexander Denton, of Hillesden, in the County of Buckingham, and Anne his wife, Dowghter and Heyr of Richard Willyson of Suggerwesh in the Countie of Hereford; which Anne deceased the 29th of October, A.D. 1566 the 18th yere of her Age, the 23rd of his Age."

"But," says Browne Willis, "this was but a cænotaph, for Alexander Denton, the husband, who lived some years after, and marry'd another lady, was bury'd with her at Hillesden, Co. Bucks; where he died January the 18th, 1576."

Under the south window is an effigy of Bishop Trevenant (1389-1404), the builder of the Perpendicular alterations in this transept. The effigy is unfortunately headless and has lost its hands. The feet are resting on a lion.

There is a brass to T. Smith, organist of the Cathedral (1877).

The remains of an ancient fireplace may be noticed on the west side of the south transept.

They consist of a rectangular recess with chimney vault behind. This was doubtless cut away when the Perpendicular window was placed above on this side.

From this transept a beautiful side view is obtained of the lantern arches.

The **Organ**, which occupies the first archway on the south side of the choir, contains work by Renatus Harris. Mr. Phillips Bevan[1] writes of it, "It was the gift of Charles II., and was very nearly destroyed by the fall of the central tower. It has twice been enlarged since, once by Gray and Davidson, and lastly by Willis. It has 16 great organ stops, 11 swell, 7 choir, 7 solo, 8 pedals, with 2672 pipes. A great feature in Willis's improvements is the tubular pneumatic

[1] *Guide to the Wye and its Neighbourhood*, by the late G. Phillips Bevan, F.S.S.

EAST WALL OF THE SOUTH TRANSEPT.

action, which does away with trackers and other troublesome internals. Sir F. Gore Ouseley having been precentor of the Cathedral, it goes without saying that he made everything about the organ as nearly perfect as possible, and, for the matter of that, no lover of music should omit to hear the *Unaccompanied* service usually held on Friday morning."

In the south wall of the south choir-aisle are four Decorated arched recesses containing four effigies of bishops, belonging to the Perpendicular period. These effigies have been attributed, beginning from the west, to R. de Melun, 1167; Robert De Bethune (died 1148), the last Norman builder; Hugh Foliot (died 1234) or Robert Foliot (died 1186); and William De Vere (died 1199).

On the north wall under an arch opening to the choir is the tomb of Bishop De Lorraine or Losinga (died 1095), who superintended the building of the fine west front of the cathedral so unfortunately destroyed. This effigy also belongs to the Perpendicular period. The large size of the ball-flower and fine wood-carving of the Decorated period on these tombs is noticeable.

Between the two eastern piers of the choir is the fine effigy and brass to Bishop Mayhew, of Magdalen College (1504-1516). The effigy is wearing a mitre, and is fully vested. In front of the monument are panels filled with figures of saints, and over the effigy is an elaborate canopy, which has been restored.

In the last bay to west of the south choir aisle a door gives access to two Norman rooms, used as vestries or robing rooms, to enter which you pass beneath the bellows of the organ. Exhibited in cases in one of these rooms are some of the treasures of the cathedral, ancient copies of the Scriptures, chalices, rings, etc., described in detail towards the close of this section. A two-storied eastern chamber was added to the Norman work in the Perpendicular period, and was used as the cathedral treasury.

Before leaving the south choir aisle the old stained glass windows with figures restored by Warrington should be noticed, and the celebrated **Map of the World** is well worth some study. It was discovered under the floor of Bishop Audley's Chapel during the last century, and appears from internal evidence to have been probably designed about 1314 by a certain Richard of Haldingham and of Lafford (Holdingham and Sleaford in Lincolnshire).

> "Tuz ki cest estorie ont
> Ou oyront, oy luront, ou veront,
> Prient à Jhesu en deyté
> De Richard de Haldingham e de Lafford eyt pité
> Ki l'at fet e compassé
> Ke joie en cel li seit doné."

Prebendary Havergal says: "It is believed to be one of the very oldest maps in the world, if not the oldest, and it is full of the deepest interest. It is founded on the cosmographical treatises of the time, which generally commence by stating that Augustus Caesar sent out three philosophers, Nichodoxus, Theodotus, and Polictitus, to measure and survey the world, and that all geographical knowledge was the result. In the left-hand corner of the map the Emperor is delivering to the philosophers written orders, confirmed by a handsome mediæval seal. The world is here represented as round, surrounded by the ocean. At the top of the map is represented Paradise, with its rivers and trees; also the eating of the forbidden fruit and the expulsion of our first parents. Above is a remarkable representation of the Day of Judgment, with the Virgin Mary interceding for the faithful, who are seen rising from their graves and being led within the walls of heaven.

"The map is chiefly filled with ideas taken from Herodotus, Solinus, Isidore, Pliny, and other ancient historians. There are numerous figures of towns, animals, birds, and fish, with grotesque customs, such as the mediæval geographers believed to exist in different parts of the world; Babylon with its famous tower; Rome, the capital of the world, bearing the inscription '*Roma, caput mundi, tenet orbis frena rotundi*'; and 'Troy as '*civitas bellicosissima.*' In Great Britain most of the cathedrals are mentioned; but of Ireland the author seems to have known very little.

"Amongst the many points of interest are the columns of Hercules, the Labyrinth of Crete, the pyramids in Egypt, the house of bondage, the journeys of the Children of Israel, the Red Sea, Mount Sinai, with a figure of Moses and his supposed place of burial, the Phœnician Jews worshipping the molten image, Lot's wife," etc.

Bishop's Cloisters. -At the eastern end of the south

nave aisle a door opens to the cloisters connecting the cathedral with the episcopal palace. In the cloister is placed a monument and inscription to Colonel John Matthews of Belmont, near Hereford, who died 1826. The subject, "Grief consoled by an Angel," is carved in Caen stone.

Other monuments are: - one to the Hon. Edward Grey, D.D., formerly Bishop of Hereford, 1832 to 1837. He died July 1837, and is buried beneath the bishop's throne. A monument to Bishop George Isaac Huntingford, D.D., 1815 to 1832. He died in his eighty-fourth year, April 1832, and was buried at Compton, near Winchester. Also a monument to Dr. Clarke Whitfield, an organist of the cathedral.

The following inscription, on an ancient brass, affixed to a gravestone near the west part of the cathedral, which, being taken off, was kept in the city tolsey or hall for some time until it was finally fastened to a freestone on the west side of the Bishop's Cloisters :—

"Good Christeyn People of your Charite
That here abide in this transitorye life.
For the souls of Richard Philips pray ye
And also of Anne his dere beloved wife,
Which here togeder continued without stryfe
In this Worshipful City called Hereford by Name.
He being 7 times Mayer and Ruler of the same :
Further, to declare of his port and fame,
His pitie and compassion of them that were in woe,
To do works of charitie his hands were nothing lame.
Throughe him all people here may freely come and goe
Without paying of Custom, Toll, or other Woe.
The which Things to redeme he left both House and Land
For that intent perpetually to remain and stand.
Anne also that Godlye woman hath put to her Hand,
Approving her Husband's Acte, and enlarging the same.
Whyche Benefits considered all this Contry is band
Entirely to pray for them or ellis it were to blame.
Now Christe that suffered for us all Passion, Payne, and Shame,
Grant them their Reward in Hevyn among that gloriouse Company.
There to reigne in Joy and Blyss with them eternally !
                                            Amen."

The South-east Transept, lying between the retro-choir and the chapter-house, into which it opens, is in the main Decorated, though its window tracery is perhaps somewhat later, being almost flamboyant in character. It was altered from the original Norman apse, and in the walls bases of the earlier work remain. It has an eastern aisle, separated from it by a single octagonal pillar.

Before the aisles were added the now open window looking into the Lady Chapel formed part of the outside wall of the chapel, and was glazed. There is a lovely view from this transept, looking slantwise into the Lady Chapel. In this transept are a number of fragments of brasses, mouldings, stone, etc. The chief monument is that to Bishop Lewis Charleton, 1369. His effigy lies under the wall dividing the transept from the vestibule of the Lady Chapel. Above it is a fine monument, restored in 1875, to Bishop Coke, died 1646. This bishop was brother to Sir John Coke, Secretary of State to Charles I. His coloured shield is borne by two angels.

A black marble slab, in excellent preservation, marks the spot where the remains of Bishop Ironside were laid on Christmas Eve, 1867, in presence of the dean, archdeacon, and praecentor, in a vault specially prepared for them ; and there is a small brass on the wall. Gilbert Ironside, D.D., Warden of Wadham College, Oxford, was Vice-Chancellor of the University in 1687, when James II. seized upon the venerable foundation of Magdalen College and sent his commissioners to Oxford to expel the Fellows.

In his replies to the king, Dr. Ironside showed a firm and resolute spirit in defence of the rights of Oxford. His refusal to dine with the commissioners on the day of the Magdalen expulsion is described thus by Macaulay : "I am not," he said, "of Colonel Kerke's mind. I cannot eat my meals with appetite under a gallows."

The brave old Warden of Wadham was not left to "eat his meals" much longer in his beautiful college hall. William III., almost immediately after his accession, made him Bishop of Bristol, whence he was translated to Hereford, and, dying in 1701 at the London residence of the Bishops of Hereford, in the parish of St. Mary Somerset, was buried in that church.

It was at the instigation of the Warden and Fellows of Wadham College that the Dean and Chapter of Hereford consented to the proposal that the remains and marble slab should be removed to the precincts of their cathedral.

St. Mary Somerset, Thames Street, was the first church closed under the Bishop of London's Union of Benefices Act, and when it was dismantled and the dead removed from their vaults in the autumn of 1867, the remains of Bishop Ironside were found encased in lead only, all the outer coffins in the vault having been previously removed or stolen.

For the purpose of identification the lead coffin was opened by the Burial Board authorities, "and," says Mr. Havergal, "so perfect were the remains that the skin was not broken, and the features of the placid-looking bishop were undisturbed." In a square recess on the east wall is a bust which has been taken by various critics to be Hogarth, Cowper, Garrick, and others, but is in reality a portrait of a Mr. James Thomas, a citizen of Hereford, who is buried near this place. Under it is a brass to Sir Richard Delabere, 1514, his two wives and twenty-one children: the inscription is as follows:

"Of your Charitie pray for the Soul of Sir Richard Delabere, Knight, late of the Countie of Hereford; Anne, daughter of the Lord Audley, and Elizabeth, daughter of William Mores, late sergeant of the hall to King Henry VII., wyves of the said Sir Richard, whyche decessed the 20th day of July, A.D. 1513, on whose souls Jesu have mercye. Amen."

The north-east window contains stained glass to the memory of Bishop Huntingford. There is also an old effigy supposed to represent St. John the Baptist.

The Lady Chapel.—The elaborate and beautiful Early English work of this chapel, which dates from the first half of the thirteenth century, about 1220, was twice under the restorers' hands, the eastern end and roof having been rebuilt by Cottingham and the porch and Audley Chapel by Sir G. G. Scott. It is 24 by 45 feet in extent and has three bays. On the north side each of these bays contains two large windows, and on the south side two of the bays contain each two windows, while the third is filled by the Audley Chapel.

In 1841 the eastern gable of the chapel was stated by Professor Willis to be in a parlous state, and the rebuilding of this portion was one of the first works undertaken by Mr. Cottingham. Sir G. G. Scott completed the pavement and other restorations.

The glorious east window consists of five narrow lancets recessed within arches supported by clustered shafts, the wall above being perforated with five quatrefoil openings, of which the outside ones are circular and the centre three are oval.

Fergusson[1] remarks: "Nowhere on the Continent are such combinations to be found as the Five Sisters at York, the east end of Ely, or such a group as that which terminates the east end of Hereford."

Of the beauties and interesting features which were developed by the clearing of the Lady Chapel by Mr. Cottingham, Dean Merewether wrote:

"Its symmetrical proportions, before completely spoilt; the remnants of its ancient painting, which were traceable beneath

Photochrom Co., Ld., Photo.
THE LADY CHAPEL.

the whitewash; the fair disclosure of the monuments of Joanna de Kilpec, a benefactress to this very edifice, and Humphry de Bohun, her husband, both of exceeding interest; the discovery of two aumbries, both walled up, but one with the stones composing it reversed; the double piscina on the south side, the chapel of Bishop Audley; but especially two of the most beautiful specimens of transition arches which can be found in any edifice, bearing the Early English form, the shafts and capitals and the lancet-shaped arch above, but ornamented

[1] *History of Architecture*, ii. 38.

THE INTERIOR OF THE CATHEDRAL. 61

in their soffits with the Norman moulding, and the zig-zag decoration, corresponding with the remarkable union of the Norman intersecting arches on the exterior of the building, with

SECTION THROUGH LADY CHAPEL AND CRYPT.

its pointed characteristics. The appearance of the central column with a base in the Early English and its capital with the Norman ornament might be added : the stairs to the crypt, and the discovery of several most interesting relics in the adjoining vaults opened in reducing the floor to its original level."

It was as a memorial to Dean Merewether, to whom the cathedral owes so much, that the stained glass designed by Cottingham was placed in the east windows in the narrow lancets that he loved so dearly. It represents scenes in the early life of the Virgin and the life of Christ; the last being the supper in the house of Mary and Martha. In the side windows the visitor should especially notice the rich clustered shafts and arches, the Early English capitals, and the ornamentation of the arches. Above these windows, corresponding to the openings above the east window, a quatrefoil opening enclosed by a circle pierces the wall. The quadripartite vaulting springs from slender shafts, which descend upon a slightly raised base.

ARCH DISCOVERED AT ENTRANCE OF LADY CHAPEL.

The double piscina and aumbry south of the altar are restorations necessitated by the dilapidated state of the originals.

Monuments in the Lady Chapel.—Of great beauty and interest is the Perpendicular recess in the central bay on the north side of the Lady Chapel, in which is the recumbent effigy which tradition has assigned without evidence to Humphrey de Bohun, Earl of Hereford, who died in the 46th year of the reign of Edward III., 1372. He was, however, buried in the north side of the Presbytery in Walden Abbey, Essex.

The Rev. Francis Havergal considers this to be the monument of Peter, Baron de Grandisson, who died 1358. In any case, the knight was probably one of the Bohun family, and husband of the lady whose effigy lies under an arch in the wall adjoining. The costume is of the earlier part of the fourteenth century ; full armour, and covered (a rare example) by a cyclass, a close linen shirt worn over the armour in Edward III.'s reign. This shirt is cut short in front and about 6 inches longer behind. The visitor should also notice the fringed poleyns at the knees.

The upper story of the recess itself has open tabernacle-work, now containing a series of figures representing the crowning of the Virgin ; on one side are figures of King Ethelbert and St. John the Baptist, and on the other St. Thomas à Becket (with double crozier) and Bishop Thomas de Cantilupe. Of these, however, only the two central carvings are in their original positions, the others having been discovered by Mr. Cottingham when the oak choir-screen was removed.

In the easternmost bay on this side is the tomb of Joanna de Bohun, Countess of Hereford, 1327. To quote from Dean Merewether: "The effigy of the lady, there can be scarcely a doubt, represents 'Johanna de Bohun, Domina de Kilpec.' She was the sister and heiress of Alan Plonknett or Plugenet of Kilpec, in the county of Hereford, a name distinguished in the annals of his times : and of his possessions, his sister doing her homage, had livery 19 Edward II.

"In 1327 Johanna de Bohun gave to the Dean and Chapter of Hereford, the church of Lugwardyne, with the chapels of Llangarren, St. Waynards and Henthland, with all the small chapels belonging to them, which donation was confirmed by the king by the procurement and diligence of Thomas de Chandos, Archdeacon of Hereford ; and the Bishop of Hereford further confirmed it to the Dean and Chapter by deed, dated Lugwas, 22nd July, 1331 (ex Regist. MS. Thomæ Chorleton, Epi.): And afterwards the Bishop, Dean and Chapter appropriated the revenues of it to the service peculiar to the Virgin Mary, 'because in other churches in England the Mother of God had better and more serious service, but in the Church of Hereford the Ladye's sustenance for her prieste was so thinne and small, that out of their respect they add this, by their deeds, dated in the Chapter at Hereford, April 10th, 1333.' (Harl. MS. 6726, fol. 109.)

"Johanna de Bohoun died without issue, 1 Edward III., 1327, the donation of Lugwardyne being perhaps her dying bequest. On the 17th of October in that year, she constituted John de Badesshawe, her attorney, to give possession to the Dean and Chapter of an acre of land in Lugwardine, and the advowson of the church with the chapels pertaining to it. This instrument was dated at Bisseleye, and her seal was appended, of which a sketch is preserved by Taylor, in whose possession this document appears to have been in 1655, and a transcript of it will be found Harl. MS. 6868, f. 77 (see also 6726, f. 109, which last has been printed in *Shaw's Topographer*, 1. 280).

SEAL OF JOHANNA DE BOHUN.

"In the tower is preserved the patent 1 Edward III., pro Ecclesia de Lugwarden cum capellis donandis a Johanna de Bohun ad inveniendum 8 capellanos et 2 diaconos appropri- anda (Tanner's *Notitia Monast.*).

"The circumstances above mentioned appear sufficiently to explain why the memorial of Johanna de Bohoun is found in the Lady Chapel, to which especially she had been a bene- factress. They also explain the original ornaments of this tomb, the painting which was to be seen not many years since under the arch in which the effigy lies, now unfortunately concealed by a coat of plaster, of which sufficient has been removed to prove that Gough's description of the original state of the painting is correct. He says, 'The Virgin is represented sitting, crowned with a nimbus ; a lady habited in a mantle and wimple kneeling on an embroidered cushion offers to her a church built in the form of a cross, with a central spire and behind the lady kneel eleven or twelve religious, chanting à gorge deployée after the foremost, who holds up a book, on which are seen musical notes and "salve sca parens." Fleur-de-lys are painted about both within and without this arch, and on the spandrils two shields ; on the left, a bend cotised between twelve Lioncels (Bohun) ; and on the right, Ermines, a bend indented, Gules.' This description was published 1786.

"By this painting there can be no doubt that the donation of the church of Lugwardine was represented ; the eleven or twelve vociferous choristers were the eight chaplains and two deacons mentioned in the patent, who were set apart for the peculiar service of the Lady Chapel, and provided for from the pious bequest of Johanna de Bohoun. The two shields mentioned by Gough are still discernible, that on the dexter side bearing the arms of Bohun, Azure a bend, Argent between two cotises, and six lions rampant, or. The other, Ermines, a bend indented, (or fusily) Gules, which were the bearings of Plugenet, derived perhaps originally from the earlier Barons of Kilpec, and still borne by the family of Pye in Herefordshire, whose descent is traced to the same source. In the list of obits observed in Hereford Cathedral, Johanna is called the Lady Kilpeck, and out of Lugwardine was paid yearly for her obit forty pence."

The effigy of Joanna de Bohun is also valuable as a specimen of costume. Its curious decoration of human heads is also noteworthy.

Over the grave of Dean Merewether, who is interred at the north-east angle of the chapel, is a black marble slab with a brass by Hardman bearing an inscription, which records that to the restoration of the cathedral "he devoted the unwearied energies of his life till its close on the 4th of April 1850."

The next monument to notice is the effigy of Dean Berew or Beaurieu (died 1462) in the south wall of the vestibule. This is one of the best specimens of monumental sculpture in the cathedral. The face, which is well modelled, and the arrangement of the drapery at the feet, are especially noticeable. There are remains of colour over the whole monument. In the hollow of the arch-moulding are sixteen boars with rue leaves in their mouths, forming a "rebus" of the dean's name.

To the west of this monument is the effigy of a priest, supposed to be Canon de la Barr, 1386.

The Audley Chantry.—In the central bay on the south side of the wall is the Audley Chantry a beautiful little chapel built by Bishop Edmund Audley (1492-1502), with an upper chamber to which access is obtained by a circular staircase at the south-west angle.

After Bishop Audley's translation to Salisbury in 1502 he erected a similar chantry in that cathedral wherein he was buried, so that the object of the Hereford Chantry as the place for his interment was of course never fulfilled.

The following is an extract taken from the calendar of an ancient missal:—"*Secundum usum Herefordensem,*" which notes a number of "*obiits*" or commemorations of benefactors, chiefly between the times of Henry I. and Edward II. "*X. Kal. Obitus Domini Edmundi Audeley, quondam Sarum Episcopi, qui dedit redditum XX. Solidorum distribuendorum Canonicis et Clericis in anniversario suo presentibus, quique capellam novam juxta Feretrum Sancti Thomæ Confessoris e fundo construxit, et in eadem Cantariam perpetuam amortizavit, etc. Constituit necnon Feretrum argenteum in modum Ecclesiæ fabricatum atque alia quam plurima huic Sacre Edi contulit beneficia.*"

The lower chamber is shut off from the Lady Chapel by a screen of painted stone with open-work panelling in two stages. The chapel is a pentagon in plan, and has two windows, while a third opens into the Lady Chapel through the screen. The ceiling is vaulted, and bears evidences of having in former times been elaborately painted.

There are five windows in the upper chamber, and the groined roof is distinctly good. The boss in the centre represents the Virgin crowned in glory. On other parts of the ceiling are the arms of Bishop Audley and those of the Deanery as well as a shield bearing the letters R.I. The upper part of the chantry, which is divided from the Lady Chapel by the top of the screen which serves as a kind of rail, may have been used as an oratory; but no remains of an altar have been found. On the door opening on the staircase is some good iron-work, and Bishop Audley's initials may be noticed on the lock.

Standing by the door of this chapel the visitor has a lovely view westward, two pillars rising in the roof and across the top of the reredos, to the right the Norman arches of the north transept, and further on still the nave.

The Lady Chapel was used for very many years as a library, and after 1862 as the church of the parish of St. John the Baptist, which surrounds the cathedral, and claimed to hold its service in some part of the building.

The Crypt is entered from the south side of the Lady Chapel where a porch opens to a staircase leading down. The porch is deeply in-set, and like the crypt itself and the

THE CRYPT.

Lady Chapel, Early English. Professor Willis points out that Hereford is the only English cathedral whose crypt is later in date than the eleventh century; the well-known examples at Canterbury, Rochester, Worcester, Winchester, and Gloucester all belonging to earlier times. A flight of twenty steps leads down to the crypt, which is now light and dry, although previous to Dean Merewether's excavations it was utterly neglected and nearly choked up with rubbish. There is another approach to it from the interior of the church.

It is 50 feet in length, and consists of a nave and aisles marked out by undecorated columns. It runs beneath the whole extent of the Lady Chapel.

This crypt having been used as a charnel-house is called the "Golgotha." In the centre is an altar tomb, upon which is a large and elaborately decorated alabaster slab, in a fair state of preservation. It bears an incised representation of Andrew Jones, a Hereford merchant, and his wife, with an inscription setting forth how he repaired the crypt in 1497. Scrolls proceeding from the mouths of the figures bear the following lines:—

> "Remember thy life may not ever endure,
> That thou dost thiself thereof art thou sewre.
>
> But and thou leve thi will to other menis cure,
> And thou have it after, it is but a venture."

At the back of the reredos is a brass to Mr. Bailey, M.P. for the county, whose bust formerly stood here, but was removed to a more fitting position in the county hall.

The Vicars' Cloisters. The entrance to the college of Vicars Choral is from the south side of the Lady Chapel. Leading from the south-east transept of the cathedral to the quadrangle of the college is a long cloister walk.

In the morning, when the sun shines upon the cloister, its richly carved roof may be best seen. The western wall, with the exception of a few mortuary tablets, is quite plain. The eastern wall is pierced with eight three-light windows, between which are the remains of small niches.

Many old vicars are buried within this cloister. The roof is of oak, the wall-plates, purlins, and rafters are richly moulded, and the tie-beams and principals are richly carved on both sides with various patterns and devices.

The Rev. F. Havergal says: "The late William Cooke acquired an immense amount of information relating to the college and the vicars in olden time. His biographical notices of them are most curious and amusing, giving a complete insight into the manners, traditions, and customs of the place." He goes on to quote from the *Lansdowne Manuscript* in the British Museum, 213, p. 333.

"Relation of a survey of twenty-six counties in 1634, by a captain, a lieutenant, and an ancient, all three of the military company in Norwich.

"Next came wee into a brave and ancient priviledg'd Place, through the Lady Arbour Cloyster, close by the Chapter-house, called the Vicars Chorall or Colledge Cloyster, where twelve of the singing men, all in orders, most of them Masters in Arts, of a Gentile garbe, have their convenient several dwellings, and a fayre Hall, with richly painted windows, colledge like, wherein they constantly dyet together, and have their cooke, butler, and other officers, with a fayre library to themselves, consisting all of English books, wherein (after we had freely tasted of their chorall cordiall liquor) we spent our time till the Bell toll'd us away to Cathedral prayers. There we heard a most sweet Organ, and voyces of all parts, Tenor, Counter-Tenor, Treble, and Base; and amongst that orderly shewy crew of Queristers our landlord guide did act his part in a deep and sweet Diapason."

The North-East Transept. This transept shows ample evidence of the original Norman plan, although its present character is Early Decorated.

Of the triple apse in which the Norman Cathedral probably terminated an arrangement similar to the eastern apses of Gloucester and Norwich Cathedrals—portions remain in the walls of the vestibule to the Lady Chapel, and in this, the north-east transept, still remain parts of the apses which opened from the choir aisles. These are somewhat later than the nave and belong to the Transition period.

After the completion of the great north transept for the reception of the shrine of St. Thomas Cantilupe, the terminal apses of the choir aisles were almost entirely removed, and the present north-east transept erected.

In the centre of this transept rises an octagonal pier which helps to carry the quadripartite vaulting. Some Norman arches in the west wall doubtless formed part of the original apse. The windows belong to the Early Decorated period. Sir G. G. Scott was responsible for the restoration of the transept.

Monuments in the North-East Transept. Under the north-west window is the canopied tomb of Bishop Swinfield. The effigy of the bishop has been lost, and in its place, which is now shown, is an unknown figure which was found buried in the cloisters. In the mouldings of the arched canopy the ball-flower ornament is again in evidence, and behind the tomb a carving of the crucifixion is still visible, though nearly obliterated by the chisel of the Puritans. The beautiful vine leaf carving at the sides has, however, been happily spared ; it is similar to the leafage on the Cantilupe shrine.

The altar-tomb of Dean Dawes, 1867, one of the most active of the modern restorers, is very beautiful. It is by Sir G. G. Scott, with effigy by Noble.

Under the north-east window is an altar-tomb of an unknown bishop. It has been assigned to Bishop Godwen, 1633, but is probably much earlier.

There is also an old stained glass window, restored by Warrington, with figures of SS. Catherine, Gregory, Michael, Thomas, and a modern one, by Heaton, to the Rev. J. Goss.

In the north choir aisle, which is entered through the original Norman arch, is an exquisite little chapel known as Bishop Stanbury's Chantry. In style it is late Perpendicular (1470). The roof is a good specimen of fan-vaulting, and the walls are panelled with heraldic bearings. Its dimensions are 8 feet by 16 feet, and it is lighted by two windows on the north side, the entrance being on the south.

At the east end are shields with emblems over the place of the altar, and the west is covered with shields in panels and tracery.

The capitals of the shafts at the angles are formed by grotesques, and over the arch on the south side are shields with emblems of St. Matthias, St. Thomas, and St. Bartholomew. The Lancaster rose is prominent in the decoration, and there is much under-cutting in the carving.

The stained windows, which form an interesting collection of arms and legends, are in memory of Archbishop Musgrave, once Bishop of Hereford, to whom there is also another window by Warrington in the wall of the aisle above the chantry, which is only 11 feet in height. The subjects are taken from the life of St. Paul.

Monument to Bishop Raynaldus, 1115, one of the chief of the Norman builders of Hereford.

In a Perpendicular recess on the left of the door opening to the turret staircase which leads to the archive room and chapter library is an effigy said to be of Bishop Hugh de Mapenore, 1219. Above is a stained glass window by Clayton and Bell, placed here as a memorial of John Hunt, organist,

VIEW BEHIND THE ALTAR, LOOKING NORTH. AFTER A DRAWING BY W. H. BARTLETT, 1830.

who died 1842, and his nephew. There is also a small brass plate at the side of the window, from which we learn that the nephew James died "of grief three days after his uncle."

In the middle bay on the north side of the choir is the monument of Bishop Bennett (1617), who was buried here. He wears a close black cap, and the rochet and his feet are resting on a lion. Across his tomb one gets a fine view of the Norman double arches of the triforium stage on the other side of the choir.

In the north wall of the north choir aisle in the first of the series of arched recesses, of Decorated character, with floral ornament in the mouldings, is an effigy assigned to Bishop Geoffrey de Cliva (died 1120), and in the same bay of the choir as Bishop Bennett's tomb is the effigy of a bishop, fully vested, holding the model of a tower. It is assigned to Bishop Giles De Braose (died 1215), who was erroneously thought to have been the builder of the western tower (which fell in 1786). This effigy belongs to the Perpendicular period, when a number of memorials were erected to earlier bishops.

In the calendar of the ancient missal "*Secundum usum Herefordensem*," previously quoted, occurs the following entry:

"*XV. Kal. Decem. Obitus pie memorie Egidii de Breusa Herefordensis Episcopi, qui inter cetera bona decimas omnium molendinorum maneriorum suorum Herefordensi Ecclesie contulit, et per cartam quam a Domino Rege Johanne acquisivit omnes homines sui ab exactionibus vicecomitum liberantur.*"

In the easternmost bay on the north of the choir is the effigy of Bishop Stanbury, provost of Eton and builder of the chantry already described. It is a fine alabaster effigy with accompanying figures. The bishop wears alb, stole, and chasuble.

Beyond the entrance to Bishop Stanbury's Chantry is a Perpendicular effigy under an arch which is assigned to Bishop Richard de Capella (died 1127).

On the chancel floor is a very good brass to Bishop Trilleck (died 1360).

In the north-east transept are the following antiquarian remains:—Two altar-stones, nearly perfect, whereon are placed:—

Six mutilated effigies of unknown lay persons, probably buried in or near the Magdalen Chapels, but dug up on the south side of the Bishop's Cloisters, A.D. 1820, and brought inside the cathedral A.D. 1862.

COMPARTMENT OF CHOIR, EXTERIOR, NORTH SIDE.

Two matrices of brasses; also a small one on the wall.

The wooden pulpit very late Perpendicular work from which every canon on his appointment formerly had to preach forty sermons on forty different days in succession.

We may also notice two rich pieces of ironwork from Sir A. Denton's tomb; the head of a knight or templar's effigy and several heraldic shields from monuments in the cathedral especially seven in alabaster now placed against the east wall.

The Choir, with its details of architecture and its individual accessories, is very beautiful, notwithstanding an unusual deficiency of light, caused by the position of the transepts, which practically intercept all light except that from the clerestory. It consists of three lofty Norman bays of three stages. The middle of the three stages has some exquisite dwarfed Norman arches with no triforium passages; but there is one in the upper stage, with slender and graceful Early English arches and stained glass at back. The vaulting is also Early English, and dates from about the middle of the thirteenth century.

The principal arches of the choir are supported by massive piers with square bases. The shafts are semi-detached and bear capitals enriched with foliated and grotesque ornament. In each bay on the triforium level a wide Norman arch envelops two smaller arches, supported by semi-circular piers on each side.

A richly carved square string course runs along the base of the triforium.

The east end of the choir was covered before 1841 by the "Grecian" screen, a wooden erection placed there by Bishop Bisse in 1717, and above it a Decorated window containing a stained glass representation of the Last Supper after the picture by Benjamin West. The improvement effected by the

COMPARTMENT OF CHOIR, INTERIOR, NORTH SIDE.

removal of this screen with its heterogeneous appendages was immense. The great Norman arch was once more exposed to view ; and, in place of the Decorated window, we now have three lancets at the back of the clerestory passage.

In describing the discoveries led up to by the removal of the old screen, Dean Merewether says : " By cautious examination of the parts walled up it was discovered that the capitals were all perfect, and that this exquisite and grand construction, the mutilation and concealment of which it is utterly impossible to account for, was in fact made up of five arches, the interior and smallest supported by the two semi-columns, and each of the others increasing in span as it approached the front upon square and circular shafts alternately, the faces of each arch being beautifully decorated with the choicest Norman ornaments. Of the four lateral arches, the two first had been not only hid by the oak panelling of the screen, but were also, like the two others, closed up with lath and plaster as the central arch ; and when these incumbrances and desecrations were taken away it is impossible to describe adequately the glorious effect produced, rendered more solemn and impressive by the appearance of the ancient monuments of Bishops Reynelm, Mayew, Stanbury, and Benet, whose ashes rest beneath these massive arches, of which, together with the noble triforium above, before the Conquest, Athelstan had probably been the founder, and the former of those just mentioned, the completer and restorer after that era."

The reredos is in Bath stone and marble, and was designed by Mr. Cottingham, junior, as a memorial to Mr. Joseph Bailey, 1850, who represented the county for several years in Parliament.

The sculptor was Boulton, and the subject is our Lord's Passion, in five deep panels occupying canopied compartments divided by small shafts supporting angels, who carry the instruments of the Passion. The subjects in the separate panels are :—1. The Agony in the Garden ; 2. Christ Bearing the Cross ; 3. The Crucifixion ; 4. The Resurrection ; and 5. The Three Women at the Sepulchre.

Above the reredos a broad spandrel left by two pointed arches springing from a central pier fills the upper part of the Norman arch. The pier itself is old, but the upper part is a restoration of Mr. Cottingham's. The spandrel is covered with modern

EAST END OF THE CHOIR IN 1841.

sculpture, as may be seen in the illustration. The subject is the Saviour in Majesty, the four evangelists holding scrolls; and below a figure of King Ethelbert.

An older representation of King Ethelbert is the small effigy on a bracket against the easternmost pier south of the choir, close to the head of the tomb of Bishop Mayo, who had desired in his will to be buried by the image of King Ethelbert. It was dug up about the year 1700 at the entrance to the Lady Chapel, where it had doubtless been buried in a mutilated condition when the edict went forth for the destruction of shrines and images.

Originally there were other representations of St. Ethelbert: on the tombs of Bishops Cantilupe and Mayo, Dean Frowcester, Archdeacon Rudhale, Præcentor Porter; in colour on the walls of the chapter-house and the tomb of Joanna de Kilpec; in ancient glass, recently restored, in a window in the south aisle of the choir; and in a stone-carving over the door of the Bishop's Cloister, and the effigy formerly on the west front.

EARLY ENGLISH WINDOW MOULDING.

Opposite the throne a slab of marble, from designs by Scott, marks the spot, as far as it is known, where Ethelbert was buried.

The Choir-stalls are largely ancient, belonging to the Decorated period. They have good canopy work, and are otherwise excellent in detail. Some of the *misereres* are quaint, among them being found several examples of the curiously secular subjects chosen for this purpose by the wood-carvers of the period.

In addition to the bishop's throne, which is of the fourteenth century, there is, on the north side of the sacrarium, a very old episcopal chair, concerning which a tradition remains that King Stephen sat in it when he visited Hereford. Be this as it may, the Hereford chair is undoubtedly of very great antiquity, and belongs to, or at least is similar to, the earliest kind of furniture used in this country. The dimensions of the chair are—height, 3 feet 9 inches; breadth, 33 inches; front to back, 22 inches. The entire chair is formed of 53 pieces, without including the seat of two boards and the two small circular heads in front.

Traces of ancient colour—vermilion and gold—may still be seen in several of the narrow bands: a complete list of other painted work which has been recorded or still exists in the cathedral has been compiled by Mr C. E. Keyser.[1]

The Cathedral Library.—The Archive Chamber, on the east side of the north transept, is also used as the Chapter Library. This room, which has been restored by Sir G. G. Scott, is now approached by a winding stone staircase.

In earlier times access was only obtainable either by a drawbridge or some other movable appliance crossing the great north window. The Library (which Botfield[2] calls "a most excellent specimen of a genuine monastic library") contains about 2000 volumes, including many rare and interesting manuscripts, most of which are still chained to the shelves. Every chain is from 3 to 4 feet long, with a ring at each end and a swivel in the middle. The rings are strung on iron rods secured by metal-work at one end of the bookcase. There are in this chamber eighty capacious oak cupboards, which contain the whole of the deeds and documents belonging to the Dean and Chapter, the accumulation of eight centuries.

Among the most remarkable printed books are: A series of Bibles, 1480 to 1690; Caxton's *Legenda Aurea*, 1483; Higden's *Polychronicon*, by Caxton, 1495; Lyndewode, *Super Constitutiones Provinciales*, 1475; Nonius Marcellus, *De proprietate sermonum*, 1476, printed at Venice by Nicolas Jenson; and the *Nuremberg Chronicle*, completed July 1493. Of the manuscripts, the most interesting is an ancient *Antiphonarium*, containing the old "Hereford Use." One of the documents attached to this volume states: "The Dean and Chapter of Hereford purchased this book of Mr William Hawes at the

---

[1] *List of Buildings in Great Britain and Ireland having Mural, etc., Decorations.* London: Dept. of Science and Art, 1883, p. 128.

[2] Botfield, *Cathedral Libraries*, 1848, p. 172. When he saw the collection it was in the Lady Chapel.

Photochrom Co., Ld., tho.o.]   THE REREDOS.

price of twelve guineas. It was bought by him some years since at a book-stall in Drury Lane, London, and attracted his notice from the quantity of music which appeared interspersed in it."

The date of the writing is probably about 1270, the obit of Peter de Aquablanca being entered in the Kalendar in the hand of the original scribe and the following obit in another hand.

The oldest of all the treasures preserved at Hereford Cathedral, being certainly one thousand years old at least, is a Latin version of the Four Gospels written in Anglo-Saxon characters.

The Rev. F. Havergal thus describes it: "This MS. is written on stout vellum, and measures about 9×7 inches. It consists of 135 leaves. Three coloured titles remain, those to the Gospels of St. Matthew, St. Mark, and St. John. Two illuminated leaves are missing—those that would follow folio 1 and folio 59. With the exception of these two lacunæ, the MS. contains the whole of the Four Gospels.

No exact date can be assigned, but several eminent authorities agree that it is the work of the eighth or ninth century.

It does not exactly accord with any of the other well-known MS. of that period, having a peculiar character of its own.

From the evidence of the materials it would appear to have been written in the country, probably in Mercia, and not at any of the great monasteries.

The text of this MS. is ante-Hieronymian, and offers a valuable example of the Irish (or British) recens on of the original African text. Thus it has a large proportion of readings in common with the Cambridge Gospels, St. Chad's Gospels, the Rushworth Gospels, and the Book of Deir.

On the concluding leaves of this volume there is an entry of a deed in Anglo-Saxon made in the reign of Canute, of which the following is a translation:—

"Note of a Shire-mote held at Ægelnoth's Stone in Herefordshire in the reign of King Cnut, at which were present the Bishop Athelstan, the Sheriff Bruning, and Ægelgeard of Frome, and Leofrine of Frome, and Godric of Stoke, and all the thanes in Herefordshire. At which assembly Edwine, son of Enneawne, complained against his mother concerning certain lands at Welintone and Cyrdesley. The bishop asked who should answer for the mother, which Thurcyl the White proffered to do if he knew the cause of accusation.

"Then they chose three thanes and sent to the mother to ask her what the cause of complaint was. Then she declared that she had no land that pertained in ought to her son, and was very angry with him, and calling Leoflœda, her relative, she, in presence of the thanes, bequeathed to her after her own death all her lands, money, clothes, and property, and desired them to inform the Shire-mote of her bequest, and desire them to witness it. They did so; after which Thurcyl the White (who was husband of Leoflœda) stood up, and requested the thanes to deliver free (or clean) to his wife all the lands that had been bequeathed to her, and they so did. And after this Thurcyl rode to St. Ethelbert's Minster, and by leave and witness of all the folk caused the transaction to be recorded in a book of the Gospels."

An Ancient Chasse or Reliquary is shown among the treasures of the cathedral, which was looked upon for a long time as a representation of the murder of St. Ethelbert, but this is only an example of the many traditional tales which modern study and research are compelled to discard. It undoubtedly represents the martyrdom of St. Thomas of Canterbury. On the lower part is the murder; on the upper, the entombment of the saint, very similar in style to the later Limoges work of the thirteenth century.

The Rev. Francis Havergal gives a detailed description, which we have condensed to the following:—

This reliquary consists of oak, perfectly sound, covered with copper plates overlaid with Limoges enamel. It is $8\frac{1}{4}$ inches high, 7 long and $3\frac{1}{2}$ broad. The back opens on hinges and fastens with a lock and key, and the upper part sloped so as to form an acutely-pointed roof; above this is a ridge-piece; the whole rests on four square feet. Front of Shrine:—Here are two compartments; the lower one shows on the right side an altar, of which the south end faces the spectator; it is supported on four legs and has an antependium. Upon the altar stands a plain cross on a pyramidal base, and in front of it a chalice covered with a paten. Before, or technically speaking, in the midst of the altar stands a bishop celebrating mass, having both hands extended towards the chalice, as if he were about to elevate it. He has curly hair and a beard and moustache. He wears a low mitre, a chasuble, fringed maniple, and an alb.

In the top right-hand corner is a cloud from which issues a hand pointing towards the figure just described.

Behind, to the left, stand three figures. The foremost has just thrust the point of a large double-edged sword, with a

ANCIENT RELIQUARY IN THE CATHEDRAL.

plain cross hilt, through the neck of the bishop from back to front.

The upper compartment represents the entombment of the bishop. The middle of the design is occupied by an altar tomb, into which the body, swathed in a diapered winding-sheet, is being lowered.

The ends of the bier are supported by two kneeling figures.

On the side of the tomb furthest from the spectator is a bishop or abbot without the mitre looking toward a figure on his right, who carries a tablet or open book with some words upon it.

At either extremity of this panel stands a figure censing the corpse with a circular thurible.

The border of each compartment is formed by a double inverted pattern of gold and enamel. The ridge-piece is of copper perforated with eight keyhole ornaments.

The back of the shrine is also divided into two compartments, and is decorated with quatrefoils.

It is pierced in the middle of the upper border by a keyhole communicating with a lock on the inside.

The right-hand gable is occupied by the figure of a female saint. The left gable is occupied by the figure of a male saint.

A border of small gilt quatrefoils on a chocolate ground runs round the margins of the two ends and four back plates.

Those parts of the copper plates which are not enamelled gilded, while the colours used in the enamelling are blue, are light-blue, green, yellow, red, chocolate, and white.

In the interior, on that side to which the lower front plate corresponds, is a cross *pattée fitchée* painted in red upon oak, which oak bears traces of having been stained with blood or some other liquid. The wood at the bottom is evidently modern. This reliquary is said to have been originally placed upon the high altar. It appears to have been preserved by some ancient Roman Catholic family until it came into the possession of the late Canon Russell, and bequeathed by him to the authorities of the cathedral.

The art of enamelling metals appears to have been introduced from Byzantium through Venice into Western Europe at the close of the tenth century. After this time Greek artists are known to have visited this country, and to have carried on a lucrative trade in the manufacture of sacred vessels, shrines, etc.

Ancient Gold Rings. One of pure gold, supposed to have been worn by a knight templar, was ploughed up near Hereford. The device on the raised besel is a cross pattée in a square compartment, on each side of which are a crescent and a triple-thonged scourge.

Within the hoop is engraved in black-letter character "*Sancte Michael.*" Date about 1380.

A massive ring set with a rough ruby of pale colour was found in the tomb of Bishop Mayew. On each side a bold tan cross with a bell is engraved. These were originally filled with green enamel. Inside is engraved and enamelled "Ave Maria."

A superb ring was also found in Bishop Stanbury's tomb, on the north side of the altar. It contains a fine and perfect sapphire, and flowers and foliage are beautifully worked in black enamel on each side of the stone.

A fine gold ring was discovered in Bishop Trilleck's grave in 1813, but was stolen in 1838 from the cathedral. It was never recovered, though £30 was offered as a reward.

The Stained Glass has survived only in a few fragments, scattered about the eastern end of the cathedral.

Some of the best, apparently of early fourteenth century date, is in one of the lancets on the south side of the Lady Chapel, west of the Audley Chapel. The subjects are:
1. Christ surrounded by symbols of the four evangelists; 2. Lamb and flag; 3. Angel and Maries at the sepulchre; 4. Crucifixion; 5. Christ bearing His cross.

In the north-east transept is an ancient glass window, restored and entirely releaded by Warrington, at the cost of the Dean and Chapter, Oct. 1864. It is a fairly good specimen of fourteenth century work. For many years it was hidden away in old boxes, and was formerly fixed in some of the windows on the south side of the nave.

The figures represent—1. St. Katherine; 2. St. Michael; 3. St. Gregory; 4. St. Thomas of Canterbury.

In the south-east transept, again, is a window of ancient glass, erected under the same circumstances. The figures in this case represent—1. St. Mary Magdalene; 2. St. Ethelbert; 3. St. Augustine; 4. St. George.

In the north aisle of the nave is a two-light window by Warrington. It was erected in 1862 by Archdeacon Lane Freer to the memory of Canon and Mrs. Clutton. The subjects are from the life of St. John the Baptist.

In the north transept is a very fine memorial window to Archdeacon Lane Freer, erected at a cost of £1316. The window is one of the largest of the Geometric period (*temp.*

Edward I.) in England, the glass being 48 feet 6 inches in height by 21 feet 6 inches in breadth. About five or six shades each of ruby and Canterbury blue are the dominating colours. Plain white glass has also been wisely used in the upper part of the window. It was designed and erected by Messrs. Hardman.

There is a small window by Clayton and Bell in the north aisle of the choir to the memory of John Hunt, organist of the cathedral. The subjects, in eight medallions, are :—1, 2. King David ; 3, 4. Jubal ; 5, 6. Zachariah the Jewish Priest ; 7. St. Cecilia ; 8. Aldhelm. In Bishop Stanbury's Chapel is

MONUMENTAL CROCKET.

EARLY ENGLISH BASEMENT MOULDING.

a memorial window to Archdeacon Musgrave, of which the subjects are :—1. St. Paul present at the Martyrdom of S. Stephen ; 2. Conversion of St. Paul ; 3. The Apostle consecrating Presbyters ; 4. Elymas smitten with Blindness. In the lower part of the window, 5. Sacrifices to Paul and Barnabas at Lystra ; 6. St. Paul before the Elders at Jerusalem ; 7. His Trial before Agrippa ; 8. His Martyrdom.

The five eastern windows in the Lady Chapel were designed by Mr. Cottingham, junior, and executed by Gibbs, to the memory of Dean Merewether.

A series of twenty-one subjects, in medallions, connected

THE INTERIOR OF THE CATHEDRAL.   89

with the life of our Lord. These windows were erected in 1852.

In the south-east transept is a memorial window to Bishop Huntingford, 1816 to 1832. It was designed and manufactured by Warrington at the sole cost of Lord Saye and Sele.

The upper part of the tracery is filled with the arms of George III., those of the See of Gloucester, the See of Hereford, Winchester College, and of the bishop's family.

The subjects, relating to St. Peter, are :—
1. His Call ; 2. Walking on the Sea ; 3. Receiving the Keys : 4. Denial of our Lord ; 5. S. Peter and S. John at the Gate of the Temple ; 6. Baptism of Cornelius ; 7. Raising of Dorcas : 8. Deliverance from Prison by an Angel.

In the north and south side of the clerestory of the choir are simple stained glass windows, consisting of various patterns. They were manufactured by Messrs. Castell of Whitechapel.

The eastern central window of the choir was an anonymous gift in 1851, executed by Hardman.

Its beauties are entirely lost at its present height from the ground. The circular medallions are 3 feet in diameter, the subjects being : —
1. The Ascension ; 2. The Resurrection ; 3. The Crucifixion.

The upper semi-circles represent Christ healing lepers and demoniacs; the lower, His being taken down from the Cross, and Mary with the box of precious ointment.

CHAPTER IV.

HISTORY OF THE SEE.

THE true origin of the See of Hereford is lost in remote antiquity. However, it seems probable from the researches of many antiquarians that when Putta came to preside here in the seventh century the see was re-established.

The Rev. Francis Havergal writes on this matter in the beginning of his *Fasti Herefordenses*.

"The Welsh claim a high antiquity for Hereford as the recognised centre of Christianity in this district. Archbishop Usher asserts that it was the seat of an Episcopal See in the sixth century, when one of its bishops attended a synod convened by the Archbishop of Caerleon (A.D. 544). In the *Lives of the British Saints* (Rev. W. J. Reeves, 1853), we learn that Geraint ab Erbin, cousin of King Arthur, who died A.D. 542, is said to have founded a church at Caerffawydd, the ancient British name for Hereford. In Wilkin's *Concilia*, 1. 24, it is recorded that beyond all doubt a Bishop of Hereford was present at the conference with St. Augustine, A.D. 601. Full particulars are given of the supposed time and place of this conference. It is also stated—'*In secunda affuisse perhibentur septem hi Britannici episcopi Herefordensis, Tavensis alias Llantavensis, Paternensis, Banchoriensis, Chirensis alias Elinensis, Uniacensis alias Wiccensis, Morganensis.*' It is styled '*Synodus Wigornensis*,' or according to Spelman, '*Pambritannicam*.' Nothing whatever is known of the names or of the number of British bishops who presided over the earliest church at Hereford."

The boundaries of this diocese in the tenth century are defined in Anglo-Saxon in an ancient volume known as the *Mundy Gospels*, now in the library of Pembroke College, Cambridge.

"The condition of the Church of Hereford (*circa* 1290 A.D.) gave clear testimony to the liberal piety of its founders by the extensiveness of its lands. The diocese itself was richly endowed by nature, and enviably situated. Those of St. Asaph, Lichfield, Worcester, Llandaff, and St. David's, were its neighbours. On the north it stretched from where the Severn enters Shropshire to where that river is joined on the south by the influx of the Wye. From the west to the east perhaps its greatest width might have been found from a point where the latter river, near Hay, leaves the counties of Radnor and Brecon, by a line drawn to the bridge at Gloucester. It embraced portions of the counties of Radnor, Montgomery, Salop, Worcester, and Gloucester, and touched upon that of Brecon. It included the town of Monmouth, with four parishes in its neighbourhood. The Severn environed its upper part. Almost midway it was traversed by the Teme, and the Wye pursued its endless windings through the lower district,—a region altogether remarkable for its variety, fertility, and beauty, abounding in woods and streams, rich pastures, extensive forests, and noble mountains. In several of the finest parts of it Episcopal manors had been allotted, furnishing abundant supplies to the occupiers of the see."[1]

In the early history of British dioceses, territorial boundaries were so vague as to be scarcely definable, but one of the earliest of the bishops holding office prior to the landing of Augustine was one Dubric, son of Brychan, who established a sort of college at Hentland, near Ross, and later on removed to another spot on the Wye, near Madley, his birthplace, being guided thither by the discovery of a white sow and litter of piglings in a meadow; a sign similar to the one by which the site of Alba Longa was pointed out to the pious son of Anchises.

Dubric probably became a bishop about 470, resigned his see in 512, and died in Bardsey Island, A.D. 522.

It was this Dubric who is said to have crowned Arthur at Cirencester, A.D. 506. When he became bishop he moved to Caerleon, and was succeeded there by Dewi, or David, who removed the see to Menevia (St. David's).

The Saxons were driving the British inhabitants more and more to the west, and before the close of the sixth century they

[1] Rev. J. Webb's *Roll of the Household Expenses of Bishop Swinfield*, xviii.

had founded the Mercian kingdom, reaching beyond the Severn, and in some places beyond the Wye.

The See of Hereford properly owes its origin to that of Lichfield, as Sexwulf, Bishop of that diocese, placed at Hereford Putta, Bishop of Rochester, when his cathedral was destroyed by the Mercian King Ethelred.

From Bede we learn that in 668 A.D. Putta died, and that one Tyrhtel succeeded him, and was followed by Torhtere.

Wahlstod, A.D. 731, the next Bishop, is referred to by both Florence of Worcester and William of Malmsbury, as well as Bede. We also hear of him in the writings of Cuthbert, who followed him in 736. Cuthbert relates in some verses that Wahlstod began the building of a great and magnificent cross, which he, Cuthbert, completed.

Cuthbert died, A.D. 758, and was followed by Podda, A.D. 746. The names of these early Bishops cannot all be regarded as certain, and their dates are, in many cases, only approximate. Some of them may have been merely assistants or suffragans to other Bishops of Hereford.

The remaining Bishops of Hereford, prior to the Conquest, we give in the same order as the Rev. H. W. Phillott in his valuable little *Diocesan History*.

A.D. 758, Hecca.
777, Aldberht.
781, Esne.
793, Cedmand (doubtful).
796, Edulf.
798, Uttel.
803, Wulfheard.
824, Beonna.
825, Eadulf (doubtful).
833, Cedda.

A.D. 836, Eadulf.
838, Cuthwulf.
866, Deorlaf.
868, Ethelbert.
888, Cynemund.
895, Athelstane I.
901, Edgar.
930, Tidhelm.
935, Wulfhelm.
941, Elfric.
966, Ethelwolf.

1016, Athelstane II.: he rebuilt the cathedral "from the foundations";[1] but also saw it destroyed in a raid of the Welsh and Irish under Elfgar.

1056, Leofgar, slain in a fight with the Welsh.

Walter of Lorraine, A.D. 1061–1079. The diocese had been administered for the last four years by the Bishop of Wor-

[1] Anglo-Saxon Chronicle.

cester, when Queen Edith's chaplain, a foreigner by birth, Walter of Lorraine, was appointed. Beyond a probably satirical reference by William of Malmsbury, all that is known of Walter is an account of a discreditable death.

Robert de Losinga, A.D. 1079–1095. A man of much learning and ability. During his episcopate, according to William of Malmsbury, the cathedral was rebuilt after the pattern of Charlemagne's church at Aix-la-Chapelle. In his time also Walter de Lacy built the Church of St. Peter at Hereford. He was a keen man of business, and it has been suggested that he was open to bribery, but this accusation is hardly compatible

A GARGOYLE IN THE CLOISTERS. DRAWN BY A. HUGH FISHER.

with his intimate companionship with the high-minded Wulstan, Bishop of Worcester, the date of whose death, January 19, 1095, is included in the calendar of the Hereford Service-Book.

Gerard, A.D. 1096–1101. Three days after the body of William Rufus had been brought from the forest to Winchester by Purkiss, the charcoal burner, Gerard, who was the Bishop of Winchester's nephew, assisted at the coronation of Henry I., for which service it was said he was promised the first vacant archiepiscopal see. The King tried to evade the bargain a few years later by promising to increase the Hereford income to the value of that at York, but Gerard carried the day and obtained his promotion.

Reynelm, A.D. 1107-1115, Chancellor to Queen Matilda ; he resigned his appointment as soon as it was conferred, on account of the King's quarrel with Anselm on the question of investiture, was banished for six years, and was only consecrated in 1107. He is said to have been the founder of the hospital of St. Ethelbert, and continued the work in the Cathedral begun by Robert de Losinga. He regulated the establishment of prebendaries and canons living under a rule.

Geoffrey de Clive, A.D. 1115–1119. During the latter years of this episcopate, a question of jurisdiction over the districts of Ergyng and Ewias, which had begun in the previous century, was revived between the Bishop of Llandaff and the Bishops of Hereford and St. David's.

Richard de Capella, A.D. 1120-1127, King's chaplain and keeper of the Great Seal under the Chancellor. He helped to build at Hereford a bridge over the Wye.

During his episcopate the Royal Charter was granted for the annual holding of a three days' fair (increased to nine days later) commencing on the evening of the 19th of May, called St. Ethelbert's Day.

Nine-tenths of the profits of this fair went to the Bishop and the rest to the Canons of the Cathedral. The bishop's bailiff held a court within the palace precincts, with pillory and stocks. The bishop also had a gaol for the incarceration of offenders against his rights during fair-time.

Tolls were levied at each gate of the city. The suspension of civic authority during fair-time was for centuries a source of frequent quarrels. As late as the eighteenth century a ballad-singer was punished by the bishop's officers.

The wreck of the "White Ship" occurred during this episcopate (Nov. 25th, 1120), and one of the victims was Geoffrey, Archdeacon of Hereford.

Robert de Bethune, A.D. 1131–1148, had become prior of his monastery at his native place of Bethune, in French Flanders, and thence had gone to Llanthony, a priory in a glen of the Hatteral Hills in the disputed district of Ewias.

When later on the country was torn and despoiled with the bitter struggle for the Crown, Bishop Robert, who was a personal friend of Henry, Bishop of Winchester, the King's brother, sided with Stephen.

HISTORY OF THE SEE.

Hereford was seized near the beginning of the campaign by Geoffrey de Talebot, and held by him for four or five weeks for the Empress Matilda. It was then captured by Stephen, and the victory celebrated in the cathedral on Whitsunday (A.D. 1138), when the King attended mass wearing his crown, and seated, it is said, in the old chair described in an earlier chapter.

In 1139, the Empress's army again attacked Hereford, and seizing the cathedral, drove out the clergy, fortified it, and used it as a vantage ground from which to attack the castle. The tower was used as a platform, from which missiles were thrown, and the nave as a stable: while a trench and rampart was carried across the graveyard.

Bishop Robert was present at Winchester when the Empress was accepted there by the clergy, and returned thence to Hereford to purify the cathedral. He died at Chalons of a disease contracted while attending a council of Pope Eugenius III.

The Pope decided that his body should be taken to Hereford, and it was enclosed in the hide of an ox for the journey. Both at Canterbury and at London were great demonstrations of grief, which were again repeated at Ross, and on a still larger scale at Hereford. Bishop Robert was undoubtedly a great man, and his reputation for fine character, bravery, and ability was well deserved.

Gilbert Foliot, A.D. 1148–1163, the next Bishop, had been consecrated as Abbot of St. Peter's, Gloucester, by Bishop Robert, with whom he had contracted an early friendship as far back as 1139.

On the death of Bishop Robert, he was consecrated at St. Omer. He assisted at the consecration of Becket at Canterbury, and the next year was transferred to the See of London. He was followed by **Robert of Maledon**, A.D. 1163–1168, said to have been remarkably wise.

Amongst his pupils he numbered John of Salisbury. He attended the council of Clarendon, A.D. 1162, and in 1164 was present at the meeting at Northampton between Becket and the King.

Such was the fury and importance of the Becket controversy that even distant Hereford was entangled with it. Two Hereford Bishops took part in the quarrel, and it was through this that the see continued vacant for six years after Bishop Robert's death.

Notwithstanding the rigorous order of Henry VIII., A.D. 1538, for the destruction of all images and pictures of Bishop Becket, there still existed in the cathedral, till late in the seventeenth century, a wall painting of the Archbishop, and even yet in the north-east transept there remains a figure of him in one of the windows in good preservation. The enamelled chasse or reliquary, with scenes of Becket's murder and entombment, and its dark but doubtful stain, has already been described among the treasures of the cathedral.

Some four miles from Hereford is yet another memorial still remaining in a well-preserved window of painted glass at Credenhill, a part of which represents the murdered Becket. Lastly, the festival of the translation of St. Thomas of Canterbury, July 7, is still included in the cathedral calendar.

Robert Foliot, A.D. 1174-1186, had been a friend of Becket's, and may have had some share in his education.

William de Vere, A.D. 1186-1199, removed the apsidal termination at the east end of the cathedral, and is said to have erected chapels, since replaced by the Lady Chapel and its vestibule.

Giles de Braose, A.D. 1200-1215, a stubborn opponent of King John.

Hugh de Mapenor, A.D. 1216-1219, received his appointment by the influence of the papal legate, who, after King John's submission, claimed the right of nomination to all vacant sees and benefices.

Hugh Foliot, A.D. 1219-1234, founded the Hospital of St. Katherine at Ledbury, in which still hangs a portrait of him, painted from an older picture. A tooth of St. Ethelbert was presented to the cathedral during his episcopacy. He endowed the Chapels of St. Mary Magdalene and St. Katherine, in the ancient building adjoining the Bishop's palace, destroyed in the eighteenth century.

Ralph de Maydenstan, A.D. 1234-1239, presented to the see a house in Fish Street Hill, London, as a residence for the bishops when in the metropolis. He also made various gifts to the cathedral, the chapter, and the college of vicars choral. This Bishop was one of the commissioners to settle the marriage of Henry III. with Eleanor of Provence.

Peter of Savoy (Aquablanca), A.D. 1240-1268, a native of Aqua Bella, near Chambéry, whose appointment was an instance of the preference Henry III. showed for foreigners. One of the most unpopular men in England; he was hand in glove with the weak-minded, waxen-hearted King in schemes for money getting.

Bishop Aquablanca probably built the graceful north-west transept of the cathedral, containing the shrine under which lie the remains of his nephew, a Dean of Hereford, together with his own, except the heart. This was carried, as he had requested it should be, to the church he had founded in his native place.

John de Breton, or Bruton, A.D. 1268-1275.

Thomas de Cantilupe, A.D. 1275-1282. Born A.D. 1220, he showed, as a child, unusual religious zeal, was educated at Oxford and Paris, and for some years filled the office of Chancellor of England at the choice of the barons. This post he lost on the death of Simon de Montfort. When he was elected by the Chapter of Hereford to fill the episcopal chair on De Breton's death he was only persuaded to accept it with difficulty.

Bishop Cantilupe was renowned for his extreme piety and devotional habits. In a dispute concerning the chace of Colwall, near Malvern Forest, from which was derived the Bishop's supply of game, he maintained successfully the episcopal rights. He was also triumphant in a more important quarrel with the Welsh King Llewellyn about the wrongful appropriation of three manors.

When Lord Clifford was in trouble for plundering his cattle and maltreating his tenants, Bishop Cantilupe inflicted personal chastisement upon him with a rod in the cathedral. The clergy no less than laymen did he subdue, appealing when necessary to the Pope.

In a quarrel arising out of a matrimonial case, in which the defendant appealed to Canterbury against a sentence of the sub-dean of Hereford, he was at last excommunicated by the Archbishop for refusing to go to discuss the affair with him at Lambeth. At Rome he obtained a favourable decree, but died in Tuscany on the homeward journey.

As already described, his remains were finally laid with great pomp in the Lady Chapel.

Five years later the bones of Bishop Cantilupe were moved to the Chapel of St. Katherine, in the north-west transept. Twice more were they moved, finally resting in the same Chapel of St. Katherine.

Richard Swinfield, A.D. 1283-1316, the next Bishop, had been Bishop Cantilupe's devoted chaplain. He kept wisely aloof from politics, but offered a keen resistance to any infringement on the rights of his diocese. Several boundary questions were settled by Bishop Swinfield, and in 1289-90 he made a tour through his diocese, of which has come down to us a journal of daily expenses.

Bishop Swinfield was the probable builder of the nave-aisles and two easternmost transepts. In his time the "*Mappa Mundi*" came into possession of the Chapter.

He worked hard to obtain the Canonisation of his illustrious predecessor, but it was not till four years after his death that Pope John XXII. granted an act for the purpose. He was buried in the cathedral.

Adam Orleton, A.D. 1316-1327, was a friend of Roger Mortimer, and consequently was opposed to Edward II. Throughout the struggle of those many miserable years the affairs of the diocese were dragged in the mire of civil war. It was the Bishop of Hereford who, at Neath Abbey, took the King, carried him to Kenilworth, and deprived him of the Great Seal. The Queen was staying at Hereford, and thither many of the King's adherents were taken with the Chancellor and Hugh Despenser. The last-named was hanged in the town, decapitated, and quartered.

Bishop Adam showed much ability in managing the affairs of the cathedral. He obtained a grant of revenues of two churches from Pope John XXII. for monies necessary for the dedication of the Cantilupe shrine, and also for repairs in the cathedral. He was followed on his translation to Worcester by

Thomas Charleton, A.D. 1328-1343, who was made treasurer of England in 1329. In 1337 he went to Ireland as chancellor. He died in 1343.

John Trilleck, A.D. 1344-1360. The Black Death reached Herefordshire in 1349, and Bishop Trilleck is said to have kept it at bay in the city by a procession of the shrine of the recently canonised St. Thomas of Hereford.

Bishop Trilleck was buried in the cathedral, and a fine brass effigy was placed on his grave. "Gratus, prudens, pius" are among the words which may be still read from the mutilated inscription, and they appear to have had more justification than the rhetoric of the average epitaph.

TOMB OF BISHOP THOS. CHARLETON.

Lewis Charleton, A.D. 1361-1369, was appointed by papal provision. The Black Death made a second visitation in the first year of his episcopate, and it was then that the market was removed to some distance from the town on the west. The "White Cross" there placed, which bears the arms of Bishop Charleton, may mark the spot. He bequeathed money and some books to the cathedral.

William Courtenay, A.D. 1370-1375, was also appointed by papal provision, which was necessary in consequence of his youth. Although he had already held a canonry of York and prebends in Exeter and Wells in addition to the Chancellorship of Oxford University, he was but twenty-eight years of age. At Oxford he had, with Wicliff, opposed the friars, though he afterwards turned against his former ally.

John Gilbert, A.D. 1375-1389, with partial success, went to make terms of peace with Charles VI., the French King. He became treasurer of England in 1386, an office of which he was deprived by Richard II. not long before his translation to St. David's. Bishop Gilbert founded the Cathedral Grammar School.

Thomas Trevenant, A.D. 1389-1404. An active politician, this Bishop assisted in the deposition of King Richard II., and was one of the commissioners to the Pope to announce the accession of Henry IV.

Robert Mascall, A.D. 1404-1416, was employed as a foreign ambassador by Henry IV., who also made him his confessor. He attended the council of Constance in 1414.

Edmund Lacy, A.D. 1417-1420. This Bishop began to build the cloister connecting the cathedral with the Episcopal palace.

Thomas Polton, A.D. 1420-1421, was consecrated at Florence, and the next year was translated to Chichester.

Thomas Spofford, A.D. 1421-1448, Abbot of St. Mary's at York, to which post he returned on resigning his see in 1448. According to a papal bull he laid out 2,800 marks on the buildings of the cathedral, — probably completing the cloisters begun by Bishop Lacy. His pension on retiring was £100 per annum. The great west window of the cathedral was put up in his time by William Lochard.

Richard Beauchamp, A.D. 1448-1450. Son of Sir Walter, and grandson of Lord Beauchamp of Powick, he was a great architect in his day, although his chief work was done after his translation to Salisbury, when he was appointed by Edward IV. to superintend the works at Windsor which included the rebuilding of St. George's Chapel where he was buried. It is said he was the first Chancellor of the Order of the Garter.

Reginald Buller, A.D. 1450-1453, Abbot of St. Peter's, Gloucester, was translated to Lichfield. He was buried in Hereford Cathedral.

John Stanberry, A.D. 1453-1474, was a Carmelite friar at Oxford, and was chosen by King Henry VI. to be his confessor, and also first Provost of Eton. In 1448 he was made Bishop of Bangor, and five years later was translated to Hereford. After the battle of Northampton (July, 1460), he was taken prisoner and was incarcerated for some time in Warwick Castle. On his release he retired to the convent of his order at Ludlow, where he died in May, 1474. He was buried at Hereford, near his own Chantry Chapel, which still bears his name. He gave land from the garden of the bishop's palace for building a dwelling-house for the vicars choral, which was completed in 1475.

Thomas Mylling, A.D. 1474-1492, the next Bishop, was Abbot of St. Peter's, Westminster, where he had been a monk. King Edward IV. made him a Privy Councillor and gave him the see of Hereford in remembrance of his services to Elizabeth Woodville, whom he received into sanctuary when her husband had to fly to Holland. After his death his body was carried to Westminster, and the stone coffin is still there which is said to have enclosed his remains.

Edmund Audley, A.D. 1492-1502, a prebendary of Lichfield, of Lincoln, and of Wells, was Bishop of Rochester in 1480, translated to Hereford in 1492, and to Salisbury in 1502. The beautiful chantry chapel on the south side of the Lady Chapel, near the shrine of St. Thomas of Cantilupe, was founded by him. He also presented a silver shrine to the cathedral, and a pulpit at St. Mary's, Oxford, is said to be his gift.

Adrian de Castello, A.D. 1503-1504. He conducted the negotiations between Henry VII. and the Pope; and he was translated from Hereford to Bath and Wells, but never visited either see.

Richard Mayhew, A.D. 1504-1516, was made in 1480 the first regular president of Bishop Waynflete's new College of St. Mary Magdalene at Oxford. He was also Chancellor of the University, and almoner to King Henry VII., by whom he had been sent in 1501 to bring the Infanta Katharine of Aragon from Spain as the bride of Prince Arthur.

He was buried near the effigy of St. Ethelbert on the south side of the choir, where his tomb is still to be seen.

Charles Booth, A.D. 1516–1535, Archdeacon of Buckingham, and Chancellor of the Welsh Marches, left a lasting memorial in the north porch of the cathedral, which bears upon it the date of his death. He seems to have been much in the King's favour, and was summoned in 1520 to make one of the illustrious company on the Field of the Cloth of Gold. He was attached to the company of Henry's "dearest wife, the queen," and was accompanied by thirty "tall personages."

On his death he left some books to the library, as well as a tapestry for the high altar; also to his successor a gold ring and other articles which have disappeared.

Edward Foxe, A.D. 1535–1538. This "principal pillar of the Reformation," as Fuller calls him, is said by Strype to have been "an excellent instrument" in its general progress.

A Gloucestershire worthy, having been born at Dursley in that county, he was sent first to Eton and then to Cambridge, becoming, in 1528, Provost of King's College. In 1531 he succeeded Stephen Gardiner as Archdeacon of Leicester. For many years almoner to the King, he was employed in embassies to France, Italy, and Germany, the most important of these diplomatic missions being in February, 1527, when he was sent to Rome with Gardiner to negotiate in the matter of Henry's separation from his "dearest wife."

Foxe first introduced Cranmer to the King; and he, again, wrote the book called *The Difference between the Kingly and the Ecclesiastical Power*, which Henry wished people to think he had partly written himself, intended, as it was, to make easier his assumption of ecclesiastical supremacy.

In August, 1536, Bishop Foxe began, by deputy, a visitation of the diocese for the valuation of all church property therein, in accordance with the order referred to above. Dr. Coren, his vicar-general, actually carried out the valuation, and its results are to be found in the pages of *Valor Ecclesiasticus*, printed by the Record Commissioners in 1802.

In March, 1535–6, an Act was passed by Parliament granting to the King all religious houses possessing a revenue under £200 per annum. There were about eighteen houses in the diocese, excluding the cathedral, and of these only the priories of Wenlock,

Wigmore, and Leominster possessed revenues exempting them from appropriation. Bishop Foxe died in London in May, 1538, and was buried in the Church of St. Mary Monthalt.

John Skypp, A.D. 1539-1552. The Archdeacon of Leicester, Edmund Bonner, was appointed to the see on Foxe's death, but was removed to London before his consecration, and John Skypp, Abbat of Wigmore, Archdeacon of Dorset, and chaplain and almoner to Ann Boleyn, became the next Bishop.

He was associated with Cranmer, though, after Cromwell's execution for high treason in 1540, the Archbishop became distant towards him. He was the part compiler with Foxe of the *Institution of a Christian Man*, published in 1537, of the *Erudition* or *King's Book*, published in 1543, and was probably one of the committee employed to draw up the first Common Prayer-Book of Edward VI., in 1548, although, on its completion, he protested against its publication. He died in 1552 at the episcopal residence in London.

John Harley, A.D. 1553-1554, was appointed by Edward VI. to hold the see "during good behaviour." He was consecrated on May 26, 1553, but only to be deposed in March, 1554. Soon after Mary came to the throne, she appointed a commission of bishops to deprive the bishops appointed during the reign of her brother. On various charges, and especially on that of "inordinate life" (meaning marriage), the bishopric of Harley was declared void. He is said to have spent the remainder of his life wandering about in woods "instructing his flock, and administering the sacrament according to the order of the English book, until he died, shortly after his deposition, a wretched exile in his own land."

Robert Parfew, A.D. 1554-1557, also known as Wharton, was instituted to the Hereford See at St. Mary's Church, Southwark, by Lord Chancellor Gardiner. He had been Abbat of St. Saviour's, Bermondsey, as well as Bishop of St. Asaph, attended the baptism of Prince Edward, and was one of those concerned in the production of the *Bishop's Book*. On his death, September 22, 1537, he bequeathed his mitre and other ornaments to Hereford Cathedral, though whether he was buried there or in Mold Church seems doubtful. The Dean of Exeter, Dr. Thomas Reynolds, was appointed to succeed him, but was imprisoned in the Marshalsea, on the accession of Elizabeth, before he had been consecrated, and died there in 1559. Fuller, in his *Church History of Britain*, remarks: "I take the Marshalsea to be, in those times, the best for the usage of prisoners, but O the misery of God's poor saints in Newgate, under Alexander the gaoler! More cruel than his namesake the coppersmith was to St. Paul; in Lollard's Tower, the Clink, and Bonner's Coal-house, a place which minded them of the manner of their death, first kept amongst coals before they were burnt to ashes."[1]

John Scory, A.D. 1559-1585, was translated from Chichester. On the accession of Mary, 1553, he is said to have done penance for his marriage, and generally reconciled himself with Rome, then to have withdrawn to Friesland and retracted his recantation, becoming superintendent to the English congregation there. When Elizabeth came to the throne he returned, preached before her by appointment in Lent, 1558, was restored to Chichester, and later on was elected to Hereford.

During his episcopate the persuasive Queen induced Bishop Scory to surrender to the Crown nine or ten of the best manors belonging to the see, and to receive in exchange advowsons and other less valuable possessions. In these transactions it is possible he thought more of his own interest than that of his successors; in any case, serious charges were brought against him in other ways. His steward Butterfield drops into verse on the subject. One of his stanzas runs :—

> Then home he came unto our queene, the fyrst year of her raigne,
> And byshop was of Hereford, where he doth now remaine ;
> And where hee hath by enemyes oft, and by false slanderous tongues,
> Had troubles great, without desert, to hys continuall wronges.

Bishop Scory was succeeded by **Harberd (or Herbert) Westphaling**, A.D. 1585-1601, Prebendary of Christ Church, Oxford : a man remarkable for the immoderate length of his speeches, his great integrity, and a profound and unsmiling gravity. He married a sister of the wife of Archbishop Parker, and before his election to Hereford was treasurer of St. Paul's and Dean of Windsor.

According to Sir John Harrington, Bishop Westphaling was once preaching in his cathedral when a mass of frozen snow fell upon the roof from the tower, creating a panic among the

---

[1] Fuller's *Church History of Britain*, Brewer's ed., iv. 198.

frightened congregration. But the Bishop, remaining in his pulpit, exhorted them to keep their places and fear not. He spent all that he had in revenues from the see in charity and good works, leaving, says Fuller, "no great, but a well-gotten estate, out of which he bequeathed twenty pounds per annum to Jesus College in Oxford." He lies in the north transept of the cathedral, where his effigy can still be seen.

Robert Bennett, A.D. 1602–1617, a Fellow of Trinity College, Cambridge, was a famous tennis player.

Queen Elizabeth had imprisoned him for a short time for preaching against her projected marriage with the Duke of Anjou, but made him Dean of Windsor towards the close of her reign. He is said to have been vain, and especially fond of having his name and arms carved on house fronts. In 1607 the old quarrel about the Bishop's rights respecting St. Ethelbert's fair broke out again between the citizens and Bishop Bennett. He spent large sums on the restoration of the Bishop's Palace. Bishop Bennett was buried on the north side of the choir, where his tomb remains with effigy.

Francis Godwin, A.D. 1617–1633, translated to Hereford from Llandaff, which preferment he is said to have obtained from the Queen on account of his commentary *De Praesulibus Angliae.* He also wrote other historical works, including a life of Queen Mary. To quote again from Fuller, "He was stored with all polite learning both judicious and industrious in the study of antiquity, to whom not only the Church of Llandaff (whereof he well deserved) but all England is indebted, as for his other learned writings, so especially for his catalogue of Bishops." He was buried at Whitbourn, in a residence belonging to the see of Hereford, on April 29, 1633.

William Juxon, Dean of Worcester, and President of St. John's College, Oxford, was chosen to follow Bishop Godwin, but before consecration was called to London. During his episcopacy in that see, he was by Bishop Laud's procurement made Lord Treasurer of England. Fuller says of his administration of these duties that "No hands, having so much money passing through them, had their fingers less soiled therewith."

Augustine Lindsell, A.D. 1633–1634, Bishop of Peterborough, was confirmed on March 24, 1633, but in November of the following year was found dead in his study.

Matthew Wren, A.D. 1635-1635, Dean of Windsor, held a still briefer episcopate, and in the same year as his consecration to Hereford was translated to Norwich.

Theophilus Field, A.D. 1635-1636, who had been Bishop of Llandaff and of St. David's, died a year after his translation, and thereby saved the diocese the ill effects of a longer term of servile and corrupt management.

George Coke, A.D. 1636-1646, Fellow of Pembroke Hall, Cambridge, became Bishop of Bristol in 1633, and was translated to Hereford in 1636. He was a grave and studious man, and well loved in his diocese, but in the troubled days of the Civil War was deprived of his see.

Nicholas Monk, A.D. 1661-1661, who followed, was brother to the Duke of Albemarle, and provost of Eton. He died in the December following his consecration, at Westminster, where he was buried.

Herbert Croft, A.D. 1662-1671. The son of Sir Herbert Croft, of an ancient family in the county of Hereford, he was brought up at Douai and St. Omer as a Jesuit, but was restored to the English Church through the influence of Bishop Morton, of Durham. He became a determined opponent of Romanism, and wrote several treatises against it. About this time there seems to have been an appeal to the nobility and gentry of the county for help towards restoring the cathedral. Bishop Croft was buried in the cathedral, and joined to his gravestone is that of his intimate friend George Benson, the Dean. He left by his will a sum of money for the relief of widows, and for apprenticing the sons of clergymen of the diocese.

Gilbert Ironside, A.D. 1691-1701, warden of Wadham College, Oxford, was translated to Hereford from Bristol. He died in London, and was buried in the church of St. Mary, Monthalt. This church was destroyed in 1863, but the Rev. F. T. Havergal succeeded in getting the Bishop's remains and tombstone removed to Hereford Cathedral a few years later, in 1867.

Humphrey Humphreys, A.D. 1701-1712, a Welshman, was translated to Hereford from Bangor. He is said to have been a good antiquary. Again, in the early days of the eighteenth century, was the old contest revived between citizens and Bishop as to his jurisdiction in respect of the fair of St. Ethelbert. The episcopal rights remained unaltered, at least in form, down to 1838, when the privileges were taken away by a special Act of Parliament, and compensation was made to the Bishop for the profits arising from the fair privileges, to the amount of 12½ bushels of wheat or its equivalent in money value, according to the price current. This has now been transferred to the Ecclesiastical Commissioners, and the fair limited to two days' duration.

Philip Bisse, A.D. 1712–1721, translated from St. David's, was a man of great munificence, and of the best intentions, of whom it may be said he spent "not wisely but too well." He was entirely devoid of any æsthetic feeling or of architectural fitness, and in the most religious spirit committed acts of wholesale sacrilege. He employed, it is said, in the work of restoration in the palace, the stones of the chapter-house, at that time much injured, but certainly by no means ruined. He built a hideous structure intended to support the central tower of the cathedral, and as a crowning act of magnificent liberality, presented the church with the most dreadful, ponderous, and unsuitable altar-piece that could well have been devised. In an elaborate epitaph in the cathedral his virtues are recorded. It was in the time of Bishop Bisse that the meeting of the three choirs of Gloucester, Hereford, and Worcester first took place.

Benjamin Hoadley, A.D. 1721–1723, translated from Bangor, was again translated to Salisbury early in 1723. His rule over Hereford was too short for him to have influenced it for good or evil, and his history belongs rather to Salisbury and Winchester.

Hon. Henry Egerton, A.D. 1723–1746, fifth son of the third Earl of Bridgewater, was chaplain to George I. He is chiefly to be remembered for an attempt to destroy the early Norman building adjoining the Bishop's Palace, and thought to have been the parish church of St. Mary, each of its two stories containing a chantry founded by Bishop Hugh Foliot.

Lord James Beauclerk, A.D. 1746–1787, grandson of Charles II. and Nell Gwynn, a native of Hereford, was the next Bishop. It was during the last year of his episcopate on Easter Monday, April 17, 1786, that occurred the fall of the western tower of the cathedral, causing much injury. The west front of the church was destroyed, and also a great part of the nave was seriously injured. The Bishop died eighteen months after this calamity. The see was next occupied for six weeks only by the Hon. J. Harley.

John Butler, A.D. 1788-1802. By birth a German, was an active political supporter of the Government of the day.

He contributed largely to the repair of the cathedral.

Folliott Herbert Cornewall, A.D. 1802-1808. He was a member of an ancient family in the county of Hereford. Translated from Bristol to Hereford, he was again translated in 1808 to Worcester.

John Luxmoore, A.D. 1808-1815, was translated to Hereford from Bristol, and again translated in 1815 to St. Asaph. He helped to establish national schools in the diocese.

Isaac Huntingford, A.D. 1815-1832, warden of Winchester College, was translated from Gloucester to Hereford,

A GARGOYLE IN THE CLOISTERS. DRAWN BY A. HUGH FISHER.

and still continued his duties at Winchester. During his episcopate an incongruous painted window was placed by Dean Carr at the east end of the choir in 1822. He was author of several classical and theological works. He died April 29, 1832, in his eighty-fourth year, and was buried at Compton, near Winchester. There is a monument in the Bishop's cloister and a window in the south-east transept to his memory.

Edward Grey, D.D., of Christ Church, Oxford, A.D. 1832-1837. He was Dean of Hereford in 1831. He was buried in the choir of the cathedral, eastward of the throne, on July 24, 1837, aged fifty-five years. A brass plate on the wall marks the spot. There is also a monument to his memory now in the Bishop's cloister.

Thomas Musgrave, D.D., A.D. 1837-1847, Fellow of Trinity College, Cambridge; Dean of Bristol; consecrated Bishop of Hereford, October 1, 1837; promoted to the Archbishopric of York, December, 1847. He died in London, May 4, 1860, aged seventy-two years, and was buried at Kensal Green, where there is a tomb with a short inscription. In York Minster a monument in the shape of an altar tomb was erected to him,

A GARGOYLE IN THE CLOISTERS. DRAWN BY A. HUGH FISHER.

and in the north choir aisle of Hereford Cathedral are three stained-glass windows to his memory.

Renn Dickson Hampden, D.D., A.D. 1848-1868, Fellow of Oriel College; Principal of St. Mary's Hall; Regius Professor of Divinity; and Canon of Christ Church, Oxford. He was appointed in 1847 by Lord John Russell, and for the first time since the Reformation "a struggle took place between the recommending minister and a large and influential part of the clergy and laity of the church, who regarded Dr. Hampden's opinions as heretical."[1] Lord John Russell refused to with-

[1] *History of the Church of England from* 1660. By W. N. Molesworth, M.A.

draw the appointment, and it was eventually carried out in spite of all remonstrances; not, however, until the question had been taken from the Spiritual Court to the Court of Queen's Bench, where the judges were equally divided in their opinion. He died April 23, 1868, in London, and was buried at Kensal Green, close to the Princess Sophia. His scholastic philosophy was said by Hallam to be the only work of deep metaphysical research on the subject to be found in the English language.

James Atlay. A.D. 1868-1895, second son of the Rev.

BYE STREET GATE. FROM AN OLD PRINT.

Henry Atlay, M.A., formerly Fellow of St. John's College, Cambridge. He was born July 3, 1817; graduated at St. John's College, Cambridge, of which he was afterwards Fellow, appointed one of Her Majesty's Preachers at the Chapel Royal, Whitehall, 1857; Vicar of Leeds, 1859; Canon of Ripon, 1861; nominated to Hereford, May 9, consecrated at Westminster on June 24, and enthroned in Hereford Cathedral, July 2, 1868. He was succeeded in 1895 by the Right Rev. **John Percival,** D.D., the present holder of the see.

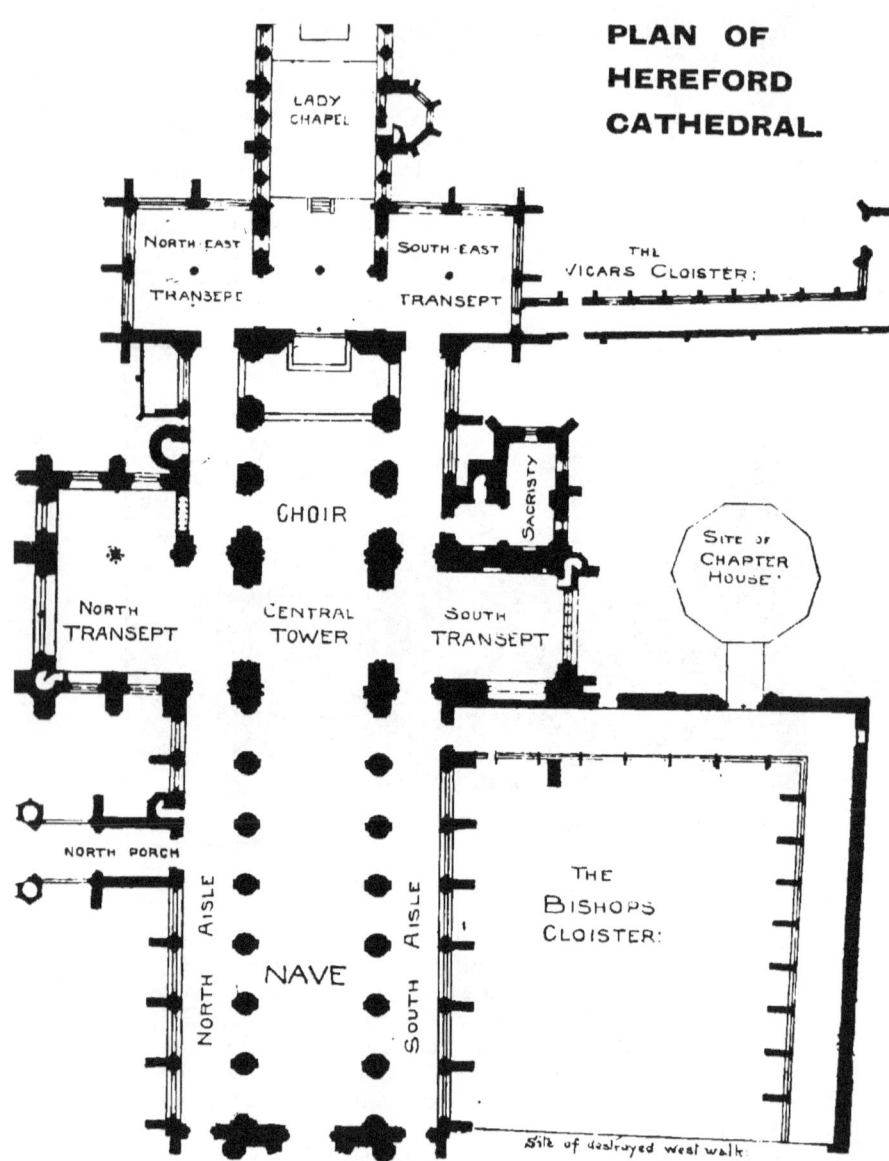

The dimensions of the cathedral are :

	Ft.	In.
Total length outside,	about 342	0
Total length inside,	,, 327	5
Length of Nave to Screen Gates,	,, 158	6
Length of Choir-Screen to Reredos,	,, 75	6
Length of Lady Chapel from Reredos,	,, 93	5
Breadth of Nave (span of roof),	,, 31	4
Breadth of Nave and Aisles (internally),	,, 73	4
Breadth of Central Transepts,	,, 146	2
Breadth of North-East Transepts (each about 35 ft. sq.),	110	6
Height of Choir,	,, 62	6
Height of Nave,	,, 64	0
Height of Lantern,	,, 96	0
Height of Tower (top of *leads*),	,, 140	6
Height of Tower (top of *pinnacles*),	,, 165	0
Height of old central timber Spire,	,, 240	0

Bell's Cathedral Series.

EDITED BY

GLEESON WHITE AND E. F. STRANGE.

In specially designed cloth cover, crown 8vo, 1s. 6d. each.

Now Ready.

CANTERBURY. By HARTLEY WITHERS. 2nd Edition, revised. 36 Illustrations.
SALISBURY. By GLEESON WHITE. 2nd Edition, revised. 50 Illustrations.
CHESTER. By CHARLES HIATT. 24 Illustrations.
ROCHESTER. By G. H. PALMER, B.A. 38 Illustrations.
OXFORD. By Rev. PERCY DEARMER, M.A. 34 Illustrations.
EXETER. By PERCY ADDLESHAW, B.A. 35 Illustrations.
PETERBOROUGH. By Rev. W. D. SWEETING. 51 Illustrations.
WINCHESTER. By P. W. SERGEANT. 50 Illustrations.
NORWICH. By C. H. B. QUENNELL. 38 Illustrations.
LICHFIELD. By A. B. CLIFTON. 42 Illustrations.
HEREFORD. By A. HUGH FISHER. 34 Illustrations.

Preparing.

LINCOLN. By A. B. KENDRICK, B.A.
DURHAM. By J. E. BYGATE.
WELLS. By Rev. PERCY DEARMER, M.A.
ST DAVID'S. By PHILIP ROBSON.
CHICHESTER.   CARLISLE.
ST ALBANS.   ST PAUL'S.

SOUTHWELL. By Rev. ARTHUR DIMOCK.
ELY. By T. D. ATKINSON.
WORCESTER. By E. F. STRANGE.
YORK. By A. CLUTTON BROCK, B.A.
BRISTOL.   GLOUCESTER.
RIPON.

Uniform with the above Series.

BEVERLEY MINSTER. By CHARLES HIATT. *Preparing.*

Opinions of the Press.

"For the purpose at which they aim they are admirably done, and there are few visitors to any of our noble shrines who will not enjoy their visit the better for being furnished with one of these delightful books, which can be slipped into the pocket and carried with ease, and is yet distinct and legible. . . . A volume such as that on Canterbury is exactly what we want, and on our next visit we hope to have it with us. It is thoroughly helpful, and the views of the fair city and its noble cathedral are beautiful. Both volumes, moreover, will serve more than a temporary purpose, and are trustworthy as well as delightful."—*Notes and Queries.*

"We have so frequently in these columns urged the want of cheap, well-illustrated, and well-written handbooks to our cathedrals, to take the place of the out-of-date publications of local booksellers, that we are glad to hear that they have been taken in hand by Messrs George Bell and Sons."—*St James's Gazette.*

"Visitors to the cathedral cities of England must often have felt the need of some work dealing with the history and antiquities of the city itself, and the architecture and associations of the cathedral, more portable than the elaborate monographs which have been devoted to some of them, more scholarly and satisfying than the average local guide-book, and more copious than the section devoted to them in the general guide-book of the county or district. Such a legitimate need the 'Cathedral Series' now being issued by Messrs George Bell & Sons, under the editorship of Mr Gleeson White and Mr E. F. Strange, seems well calculated to supply. The volumes are handy in size, moderate in price, well illustrated, and written in a scholarly spirit. The history of cathedral and city is intelligently set forth and accompanied by a descriptive survey of the building in all its detail. The illustrations are copious and well selected, and the series bids fair to become an indispensable companion to the cathedral tourist in England." *Times.*

"They are nicely produced in good type, on good paper, and contain numerous illustrations, are well written, and very cheap. We should imagine architects and students of architecture will be sure to buy the series as they appear, for they contain in brief much valuable information." *British Architect.*

"Half the charm of this little book on Canterbury springs from the writer's recognition of the historical association of so majestic a building with the fortunes, destinies, and habits of the English people. . . . One admirable feature of the book is its artistic illustrations. They are both lavish and satisfactory—even when regarded with critical eyes."— *Speaker.*

"Every aspect of Salisbury is passed in swift, picturesque survey in this charming little volume, and the illustrations in this case also heighten perceptibly the romantic appeal of an unconventional but scholarly guide-book." *Speaker.*

"There is likely to be a large demand for these attractive handbooks." —*Globe.*

"Bell's 'Cathedral Series,' so admirably edited, is more than a description of the various English cathedrals. It will be a valuable historical record, and a work of much service also to the architect. The illustrations are well selected, and in many cases not mere bald architectural drawings but reproductions of exquisite stone fancies, touched in their treatment by fancy and guided by art." *Star.*

"Each of them contains exactly that amount of information which the intelligent visitor, who is not a specialist, will wish to have. The disposition of the various parts is judiciously proportioned, and the style is very readable. The illustrations supply a further important feature; they are both numerous and good. A series which cannot fail to be welcomed by all who are interested in the ecclesiastical buildings of England." *Glasgow Herald.*

"Those who, either for purposes of professional study or for a cultured recreation, find it expedient to 'do' the English cathedrals will welcome the beginning of Bell's 'Cathedral Series.' This set of books is an attempt to consult, more closely, and in greater detail than the usual guide-books do, the needs of visitors to the cathedral towns. The series cannot but prove markedly successful. In each book a business-like description is given of the fabric of the church to which the volume relates, and an interesting history of the relative diocese. The books are plentifully illustrated, and are thus made attractive as well as instructive. They cannot but prove welcome to all classes of readers interested either in English Church history or in ecclesiastical architecture."—*Scotsman.*

"A set of little books which may be described as very useful, very pretty, and very cheap . . . . and alike in the letterpress, the illustrations, and the remarkably choice binding, they are ideal guides."— *Liverpool Daily Post.*

"They have nothing in common with the almost invariably wretched local guides save portability, and their only competitors in the quality and quantity of their contents are very expensive and mostly rare works, each of a size that suggests a packing-case rather than a coat-pocket. The 'Cathedral Series' are important compilations concerning history, architecture, and biography, and quite popular enough for such as take any sincere interest in their subjects."—*Sketch.*

LONDON : GEORGE BELL AND SONS.

www.ingramcontent.com/pod-product-compliance
Lightning Source LLC
Chambersburg PA
CBHW020125170426
43199CB00009B/649